People, Poker and Vegas:

The Journey of a Low Stakes Poker Player.

Mike Connah

Published by New Generation Publishing in 2020

Copyright © Mike Connah 2020

First Edition

The author asserts the moral right under the Copyright, Designs and Patents Act 1988 to be identified as the author of this work.

All Rights reserved. No part of this publication may be reproduced, stored in a retrieval system or transmitted, in any form or by any means without the prior consent of the author, nor be otherwise circulated in any form of binding or cover other than that which it is published and without a similar condition being imposed on the subsequent purchaser.

ISBN 978-1-80031-687-4

www.newgeneration-publishing.com

New Generation Publishing

Dedication:

'To all small stakes poker grinders everywhere - may the flop always be with you'.

Acknowledgements:

Andy Wickens: For his advice regarding the publishing process.

Ann Sermon: For putting up with me continually harping on about 'the book'.

Mark Tetlow: For his invaluable information regarding the Early Years.

Friends: For reading the earlier chapters and their considerations:

Tony Wray.

Tim Flanders.

Ray Rayter.

Authors: For allowing material from their books:

Johnny Kampis.

Marvin Karlins.

Lance Bradley.

New Generation:

For everyone involved in this book at NG for their advice and expertise.

Preface:

The desire to write this book has been festering for a couple of years, and over those years when I have regaled friends and family with my stories of poker and Las Vegas they have said: *"Mike, you should write a book"* - well here it is.

There have been many books written by professional and well established poker players over the years. Many on their poker experiences, many on the technicalities of the game and how to succeed in the diverse world of poker. Many by experienced authors turned poker players who have played the game at various levels, and many books by experienced poker players turned authors. Most of these books however discuss the intricacies of the game both from a mathematical point of view and from psychological point of view with guidance through 'implied odds' and 'variance' and other complicated issues regarding the game. There is a well known saying in the poker world 'that poker is an easy game to learn but takes a lifetime to master'. If the reader therefore wants to learn to play the game then I suggest they turn their attention to these more educational books.

I wanted to write a book from the 'little man's viewpoint'; an experienced but amateur poker player who has played poker in Las Vegas over a period of some 30 years. I have never won any large amounts of money, never been involved in high roller events, cash or tournaments, never stayed in expensive suits in top class Las Vegas hotels and never been picked up from the airport in a casino's stretch limousine. However, I believe that the thrill of playing poker in Las Vegas prevails whichever level or financial class you belong to and hope that this comes across to the reader. The book also contains some stories about the characters I have met on my trips to Las Vegas. All these stories and characters are true although some of the names have omitted or changed to protect the guilty. I want the reader to understand that poker can be fun, it doesn't have to be brutal or cruel, either financially or psychologically. It is there to be learned, and with that learning goes the meeting of a wide variety of like minded and colourful characters. The characters and the experiences noted in the book have been as equally pleasurable as the game itself.

Neither is this book a tourism invitation to visit Las Vegas, again there are many of those on the market. I want the reader to understand the Vegas can be friendly, it can be fun and it can be safe - and the truth is that it is far from that portrayed on TV or in films. It is full of pleasant, sociable Americans who just want for a break from the monotony of life for a few days of fun.

These observations are exactly what it says on the cover – true stories and real people – nothing more, nothing less. There is no chronological structure, just a pure stream of conscious and ad hoc accounts of events as they happened. On every occasion I have tried to bring instances and situations regarding poker and Las Vegas back to me on a personal level and relate them to personal experiences. In places, I have not always succeeded but that has always been my overall consideration.

Over the course of writing this book I have been amazed at the number of non poker playing friends who have agreed to read selected pages from the manuscript - solely on my request to ask them "is it of interest"? - on reading these most have politely agreed that it is, and some have even asked to read more - that is all I ask.

I also understand that many people such as my current 'lady-in-tow' (her words not mine) have absolutely no interest whatsoever in poker, gambling or casinos. If those people also find the book of interest without any thoughts of me trying to deflect them from life's straight and narrow and inviting them to venture into this magical world - again, that is all I ask - but they could give it a try!

A Poker Player's Dream

If
there is
a Heaven, please
let it be large. Long
and broad like a coalman's barge.
Let it be blushed in a quiet pastel haze
with kidney shaped tables in a deep green baize.
If there is peace and a life hereafter, may it be full
of cardroom laughter with Angels as cocktails bringing plenty
of tea, and a sign, well displayed, that Heaven is smoke free. If
there is a Heaven, let it be done out with style like Binions and
others on the four and a half mile, and let me sit down every day
of the week with the quiet and the humble, our fortunes to seek.
If there is a Heaven, I ask it be open all day, with comps and
satellite in continuous play. Let the dealer keep a good count
of the pot, with a smile on his face, and be content with
his lot. May I always have a mountain of chips and
the words 'I pass' never
stray from my
lips. If
there is
Heaven
with the
joys that it
brings, in God's
full house may I always
be dealt - Aces over Kings.

Contents Page

Acknowledgements: 1

Preface: 2

Shaped Poem: A Poker Player's Dream *Mike Connah*...4

Part I: The Early Years 7

  Chapter 1: Early Blackpool Years: 8

    'Mad' Marty Wilson: 14

    Tim and Pippa Flanders: 17

    Howard Plant: 19

    Edwina Stocker a.k.a. Rose Devine: 21

  Chapter 2: Early Vegas Years 23

    Vegas Trivia: 34

Part II: Las Vegas 35

  Chapter 1: Sin City 36

  Chapter 2: I Was There When 55

  Chapter 3: Only in Vegas 61

  Chapter 4: The Dark Side of Vegas 70

  Chapter 5: 48 Hours on Vegas Casinos 83

    Vegas Trivia 98

  Chapter 6: Getting Married in Vegas 99

Part III: Characters and Friends 103

  Chapter 1: Characters 104

    Shangai Lil 104

    Charlene the Hooker: 106

    The Perfect Retirement: 110

  Chapter 2: High Rollers 113

Chapter 3: Non gamblers 118

    Vegas Triva: 121

Chapter 4: Friends: 122

Part IV: Poker 131

Chapter 1: Shuffle up and Deal 132

Chapter 2: Poker, Gambling and Public Perception ... 138

    Poker Trivia and Quotes 146

Chapter 3: Skill, Luck, Superstition and Rules 151

    Poker Triva and Quotes 159

Chapter 4: Professionals, Semi Professionals and Amateurs 170

    Poker Trivia and Quotes 199

Chapter 5: Subterfuge, Collusion and Downright Cheating 200

Chapter 6: Beginners at the Table 207

    Final Thoughts 211

Tips: Visiting Vegas 213

Appendix 1: Ranking of the Hands in Texas Holdem 220

Appendix 2: Glossary of Poker Terms 222

Appendix 3: Texas Holdem 229

Bibliography 231

Part I: The Early Years

Early Blackpool Years
Mad Marty Wilson
Tim and Pippa Flanders
Howard Plant
Edwina Stocker a.k.a. Rose Divine
Early Vegas Years
Vegas Trivia

Chapter 1

Early Blackpool Years:

Poker and Los Vegas are inextricably linked in my world; you cannot have one without the other. My introduction to both was by chance; a twist of fate.

At one time I was involved with the Preston Magic Circle and whilst on an afternoon ramble around the Shambles in York my wife of the time bought me a second hand book with the cover showing a hand of cards, thinking it was about card magic. It was in fact *' Big Deal - a year as professional poker player'*. It was about one year in the life of Anthony Holden, who at the time was the sub editor on the Times and had taken a year out to play professional poker in Las Vegas. If only my wife had read the title of the book and not just identified the playing cards, then none of what follows would have happened - a twist of fate - I read the book in two days. It was a life changing read!

A few years later I met Tony Holden in Las Vegas at the World Series of Poker outside Binions Horseshoe casino on Fremont Street and related the story to him. He signed the book and wrote 'May the flop always be with you' on the inside cover. I think of Tony now and then whilst playing poker, and the flop is with me (see Appendix 2 for definition of 'the flop').

After the York weekend I made a few enquires and found that a poker game took place at the Tiberius casino on Station Road, Blackpool on a Saturday night. I read Holden's book again, plus other books about Texas Hold'em (see Appendix3 for definition) - the form of poker played - and I got a limited understanding of the game, and decided to go and 'have a look'. Little did I know that I would be pulled into the game that Saturday night and my world would be changed forever. I sat outside the card room with some trepidation wondering if I was allowed in to observe the game, and perhaps allowed to ask questions and learn more. After a while this well dressed lady dripping with jewellery noticed me sitting there, came up to me and asked if I played poker.

Early Blackpool Years

"Well, no" I said, *"but I would like to learn".*

"Well luvvie, we are a player short that to make up the number required for the casino to add to the prize money. If you play and make up the numbers, the winner will give you your £35 entry fee back - want to give it a try?".

I did, and was hooked for life. I was happy not to be knocked out the tournament first; I think I lasted about 2 hours into the game, but even at that first game I made some good friends and learned the general protocols and etiquette of the game of Texas Hold'em. I never did get my entry fee back from the winner!

This event bought me into a world that I had never thought existed. A world of remarkable characters that had a strange sincerity and honesty and yet an unspoken mysterious aura about them. Many went on to be good friends with whom I would play this game of poker with both in the UK and in Las Vegas. Many were consummate gamblers who would win hundreds of pounds at poker, and then lose it all in five minutes on the roulette wheel. Many were just social players who loved the company and the Saturday night game. Many went on to be professional players who made their living either through live poker or online games.

They came from every class and walk of life: from the rich who owned companies and government officials, through taxi drivers, street vendors and labourers, and others who made a living by less than honest means and to people on benefit who scrounged their money every week for the Saturday night game. There were British, Irish, French, Asian, Chinese, Cypriots, Lebanese and a multitude of other ethnicities. There were those who came with wives or girlfriends - and sometimes both! - and there were those who walked through life alone. But whatever their position in life there was one thing that bonded them together into a big, joyous, exuberant and eccentric family - their love of poker. I loved them all - and I am saddened at their passing.

In his book *'Life's a Gamble'* Mike Sexton advises anyone taking up poker:

*'........even if you have a talent and are winning at poker, if you don't **love** poker - not **like** poker, but **love** to play - don't do it, because you will be miserable'.*

Some of the characters I met in those early days - with their real names and real 'handles' were:

'Big Lizzy' and Pauline: Liz Webster was the landlady of a Blackpool B&B hotel and Pauline worked for her at the her

Early Blackpool Years

Guest House. Liz and Pauline were the exact opposites of each other. Whilst Liz was on the large (very large) side, with the exuberant nature of a typical Blackpool boarding house matron, Pauline was small, slim and often reminded me of a timid mouse. However, they always played side by side whether it be at the poker or the blackjack table. Liz bought her landlady persona to the poker table, and if you were going to beat her then you had better make sure it was with a good hand and that you had a perfect right to be in the pot. Neither was it a wise decision to try and bluff Lizzy, and if you did then under no circumstances show her your hand - or you are dead, dead as a dodo! By the same token, if she beat you in a hand, no matter how lucky it might have been, it was best to be humble and mutter the usual time honoured poker phrase: *"Good hand Liz"*.

Mazz and Dolores: Mazz was a nice affable Asian guy liked by all, and I played poker with him, drank with him and ate with him for some 20 years but still do not know his real name - given or surname! I do not even recall if he had a 'proper job' - to everyone he was just Mazz. He was clouded in mystery but I think that whatever he did it was skating very close to the line of legality and he could not have been very good at it as he was always on the scrounge and owed money to nearly every regular in the casino. He once disappeared for around 2 years and no one seemed to know where he was. On his return a few years later, he was barred from the casino for allegedly cheating - which Mazz strenuously denied. This was not at poker, but at the roulette wheel. It appears that he had formed a little cohort of friends and one of whom would distract the croupier whilst a couple more would place illegal bets on the table after the wheel had stopped spinning. It was a crude method of operation and in fact failed at its first attempt. Mazz's friends claimed innocence using their limited knowledge of the casino rules in mitigation of the offence. No official charge was made against Mazz or his friends, however, the casino banned them all including Mazz who had signed in the suspects for two years.

Maurice and Jean Dearden were ever present regulars: Maurice owned his own business, a house on the South Shore at Blackpool, and a house in Florida. He was a tall wiry man with rather a detached nature who rarely spoke. Jean however, was the opposite and was a very friendly and communicative lady. Both were good poker players, but as the night went on Jean's

Early Blackpool Years

play became more and more erratic in combination with the brandy and cokes. If they were sitting at the same table Maurice would berate her at the bad judgements and crazy plays she would make, to which Jean would reply: *"Oh, Maurice, it's only a game"*. But to Maurice, like most poker players it is not just a game and whilst not being a matter of life or death, it runs it pretty close.

Maurice was a good example of poker players who play for the love of the game not for the money but who still took it very seriously.

Arnold and Norma Gill: Norma was the woman mentioned above who got me into my first poker game - again she played for the love of the game, not for the money. She owned jewellery shops around Blackpool.

Steve 'The Womble' Walmsley: Steve sold his architect business, making him a near millionaire and jetted off to Thailand to live and play poker with the occasional trip back to UK. Steve was actually in Las Vegas with his partner when I got married in the Little White Wedding Chapel (to come later) and was a witness for me.

John 'The Viper' Prescott: John was another player who became a good friend. John is a retired chemist, and we had many a good argument/discussion on poker and all things in life generally. We made many a trip together to Liverpool to play in those early days.

Gareth 'The Nugget' Jones: Gareth was a large man who continually seemed to be on a diet. An ex finance officer with a local bank, he was one of the earliest players I was acquainted with who I would eventually watch play in the World Series of Poker (WSOP) in Las Vegas. Gareth always maintained that he taught Dave 'Devilfish' Uliett, who was one of the world's top professional players how to play poker. After a spell in Big Lizzie's guest house Gareth upped and went to live in Manila to play poker for a living. After one trip back to UK, he was refused entry back into the Philippines and lost all his worldly goods. Last I heard he was living in Cambodia, still playing poker.

Alister Findlay and Bev: Alister unfortunately passed away a few years ago. He was a hard man to like; a plain speaking Scot who upset many a poker player in those early days. He ran a home game on the North Shore at Blackpool that I played in for a couple of years. I always got on with Alister, but it wasn't easy, he was very dismissive of anyone who did not share his opinions. However, every year he would put on a charity event at the Tiberius and later on at the Grosvenor casino in Blackpool. These events would raise thousands of pounds for a local children's charity. Underneath all the bluster he was a good man, who died to early in life. Alister was another player with whom I played poker with in Vegas, at the Plaza downtown. Bev who was also a good poker player, eventually became a counsellor and we worked together for a couple of years at a prison in the North West.

During these early years of the worldwide poker boom of the early nineties a plethora of games appeared in a wide variety of venues around my local area. Pubs, clubs, homes, snooker halls; rooms were booked and a whole assortment of locations became fair game for a session of poker. One enterprising gentleman in my area transformed his garage into a card room complete with carpeting, two poker tables and lighting - entry to the game was by invitation only - I think this was a legal requirement as of course other than home games if money was involved then a gambling licence was required.

I attended many of these games in pubs and clubs, but have to be honest I was not a lover of them and rarely went back after two or three visits. I had by this time been playing poker for two or three years at the casino and had visited Vegas a few times. So, maybe I thought myself a cut above all this amateur stuff - but the indiscipline and rules and etiquette' breaking at the tables was too much for me to suffer. It was a combination of a few things: the people running these games did not know the rules and etiquette themselves, the players had never played in a casino so neither knew the rules, combine this with alcohol and it was a recipe for chaotic disaster.

The best private games in these early days were the home games ran by seasoned poker players. I ran one myself at the below mentioned Rose's home, and it was a successful game of two tables every Thursday night and Sunday afternoon. No alcohol allowed and Rose supplied the food which was included in the 'house fee' of £5. It was a small game of £30 entry with £10 re-buys for the first hour. The game ran for a couple of years until the sad demise of Rose (noted below).

Early Blackpool Years

The other game was run by Alister and Bev (noted above). Again, a well run game once or twice a week in which Alister supplied the beer which was all included in the house fee of £10 - no food; bring your own. There were usually two tables and a cash game for those knocked out of the tournament which was a £40 entry with £10 re-buys for the first hour.

Both these games had regular players who were experienced and knew the game, and this contributed to their success. It is true that many of these games in pubs and clubs led to beginners coming to the casino to play and learn the game so thereby furthering the popularity in poker in the early years. However, I also believe that it put off a lot of prospective future poker players who were concerned about the discipline and the running of the games plus the ignorance of the financial aspects of these games and poker in general.

I firmly believe that for the beginner, apart from family and home run games the only introduction to poker is via a well run casino card room. View the top class players on TV; read the books; study the game - and then visit your local casino 'to have a look'

There are many, many other characters that made up my life in those early days, too many to mention here. The last characters I want to mention are the Tetlow Brothers: Mark, Dave and Michael. Dave unfortunately passed away a few years ago whilst on a visit to his wife's hometown in Poland. Mark became, and still is, a good friend who loves his poker and blackjack and is another player who I have been with in Vegas. They, Dave and Michael especially, were good friends of Mad Marty Wilson, which leads me on to the first of the four early days characters.

Early Blackpool Years

'Mad' Marty Wilson:

Marty Wilson passed away last year at the young age of 62 and the UK lost one of its greatest and most colourful poker players. He can best be summed up in the following quotes: The first from Victoria Coren - Mitchell in her great poker book *'For Richer, For Poorer'.*

'That sparkling firework of the British Poker scene Mad Marty Wilson passed away last night. He was one of the most memorable, twinkly, mischievous, life-enhancing characters who you could ever meet who bought so much laughter and fun and will be remembered with so much love. RIP'

The second from American poker player and reporter Mike Sexton in the Poker News.

'Mad Marty Wilson made you smile just entering a room he was in. He was a true character in the poker world - one of which we'll not see again'.

I first met Marty at the Blackpool Grosvenor Poker Room. In those early days good well run poker rooms were hard to find. Marty hailed from Wolverhampton and his affection of the game we all love caused him to travel from the West Midlands to Blackpool for a game of poker. He would come up with this then girlfriend, later wife Katherine, who herself became a very proficient poker player in her own right.

Marty was at the forefront of the early days of televised poker in the UK. He started as just another player on the Channel 4 programme *Late Night Poker*. However, the producers of the programme realised very quickly his viewing appeal and made him a regular on the programme. He was not only a good poker player but a consummate gambler and was so good at fleecing the bookies that he was banned from all the major bookmaker shops in the UK, resorting to disguising himself to enter a bookmakers shop or running a team of others to place bets for him.

Early Blackpool Years

He was a great raconteur and kept the whole table in awe of some of his stories. The thing was with Marty, you never thought: *"God, I wish he would shut up"*. Despite this jovial and appealing nature, Marty was in fact an excellent poker player and went on to play poker not only in Vegas but in many other parts of the world. His biggest win would however, come in Vegas at the Rio Carnival of Poker, which he won netting himself $171,000. He later went on to teach and school people such as: Mathew Stevens (snooker player), Barry Hearn (sports promoter), Tom Cruise, Michael Greco (actors), Helen Chamberlin (TV presenter) and Phil Taylor (Darts Player).

He was such an engaging character and very generous in spirit. I was in Vegas one year with a girlfriend who later became my second wife and we met Marty and Katherine with another group of UK poker players at the bar in Binions Casino downtown. It was Marty's birthday, and everyone who sat at, or walked past that bar that afternoon (he started celebrating early) was bought a drink and invited to join the party.

On a much earlier occasion I was sitting with my first wife in the lounge bar in the Golden Nugget Casino downtown, when Marty came charging through; saw me, waved and shouted: *"Can't stop, I'm on a roll, just rushing to the loo"*. I later found out that he was at the blackjack table $5,000 to the good. He went on to win his target of $10,000 that night, which was his entry into the main event of the World Series of Poker starting next day at Binions across the street from the Nugget. The main event used to be a three day event in those days, now it is something like a week. I watched Marty play in that event; he lasted through to the second day and was then eliminated.

The last time I saw Marty was in Vegas just a few years ago. I was walking down to the World Series of Poker rooms in the Rio, when I saw him outside one of the VIP rooms just off the main poker room.

Early Blackpool Years

We chatted for a while and he said: *"Come on in and have a game of pool, it's a VIP room promoting Matchroom Sports"*. So in I went and in there was Barry Hearn and some of the known UK snooker players with whom I spent a delightful hour or so playing pool.

Marty was a true individual and he was a great supporter of local charities in his home town of Wolverhampton and hosted many charitable events, one netting £35,000 for a local charity. If you are wondering how Marty earned the nickname of 'Mad Marty', as he was such a gentleman and in no way could be considered 'mad'. Marty got the name after jumping into a Polar Bear pit at Dudley Zoo to escape local rival football fans who were chasing him. One of his other 'mad' exploits was to wager $10,000 on himself being able to drink 20 pints of Guinness in an hour. I can testify to his love of Guinness, but unfortunately I cannot testify if he won that particular bet or not. However, knowing Marty it is unlikely he wagered a bet without the odds being in his favour!

Early Blackpool Years

Tim and Pippa Flanders:

Tim and Pippa Flanders were directors and the owners of an IT software company and live not far from me in Preston, Lancashire. Tim played his poker in a similar manner to one of his computers. He was a mathematician, who talked about odds, mathematical possibilities, random possibilities etc. A quiet, pleasant man in his early forties, tall with a studious nature with glasses perched on the end of his nose and was a reasonable poker player. He went on to win large amounts of money in prestige tournaments later on in the UK and Europe and became in time an excellent poker player. Tim is another local player from those early years that went on to play in the World Series in Las Vegas. During the times in Vegas, and on other occasions of play around Europe he has sat and held his own with some of the best in the world: Phil Helmouth, Phil Ivey and Chris Ferguson amongst them.

Tim played on some of the early televised games with most of the poker celebrities of the time, including the above Marty Wilson and can count amongst his adversaries at the table the actors James Wood and Mimi Rogers (ex wife of Tom Cruise). In fact, Tim relates one story where he had to ask James Wood to: *"Shut up and be quiet",* as he was engaging Tim in conversation whilst he was in a hand - an absolute no in a poker game.

His wife Pippa accompanied him when he first appeared in the Grosvenor card room at Blackpool, but did not play and would sit quietly behind him, not speaking - just watching and learning.

Throughout the ten or so years that I knew Tim and Pippa, I never heard Pippa speak. A pleasant lady with an engaging smile, she eventually sat down to play one Saturday night. Even then, she never spoke much to the other players, just smiled - watched and learnt.

Early Blackpool Years

During the course of the years it became obvious that she was just as much a danger at the poker table than Tim and became respected by the regular players, but even then she rarely spoke, just smiled - watched and learnt.

From these humble beginnings Pippa went on the win the Party Poker World open in 2006, netting herself $200,000 and being only one of two women in the competition. Then later on she went on to win the Party Poker World Women's Open in London in 2010 winning $30,000. To this date she has won over $300,000 on the live tournament circuit, and ranks 50th in the world on the all time-time female list. A Party Poker spokesperson said this of Pippa:

'It's really exciting that Pippa's victory is the first great breakthrough for European women in poker, and demonstrates the rise of women champions around the world in open poker tournaments'.

Pippa always reminded me of another great British female player from those early days - Lucy Rokash. Lucy hailed from the Rainbow Casino in the Midlands and I watched her play on a couple of occasions in Las Vegas, once in the World Series. Lucy was a forerunner in female poker players on the world stage along with Barbara Enright, Annie Duke and Jennifer Harman. I think that is the best compliment I can pay Pippa, the local girl who can be ranked amongst some of the celebrated female poker players of the past.

However, I just think of her as I knew her in those early days at Blackpool - quiet, smiling, just watching, just learning.

Early Blackpool Years

Howard Plant:

It is rumoured that Howard came from Gypsy stock, however, I have no proof or certainty regarding that fact, but he made his money by buying up derelict buildings in Blackpool, knocking the buildings down and using the land as car parks. He also had a bookmakers licence which was passed down through his family and he would go to various racecourses on Bank Holidays - not to run a book - but to run a 'bunko booth' type of activity, enticing punters and Bank Holiday drunks to play his dartboard game. One of his associates during these times was Dave Gardner, another well known player on the Northern poker circuit. Dave's son Julian also played poker at the Tiberius and in future years was one runner up in the main event at the World Series in Las Vegas.

I have known Howard for many a year, and playing poker at the same table as Howard was always an experience - of one kind or another! He was in the same mould as 'Mad Marty', exuberant, full of life and a nonstop talker. His main claims to fame outside poker were: taking part in a BBC documentary of 2013 titled 'Summer in Blackpool', and running amok in the old Tiberius casino in Blackpool!

I was there on the second of this renowned occasions. I had been knocked out of the evening poker tournament and was sitting outside the card room which overlooked the gaming floor; a ringside seat you could say to the unfolding events.

It was the custom in those days to shout out the wager, and the number(s) at the roulette table, especially if the gambler was well known to the dealer (and Howard was). Howard's wager was around £200, and his number came up on the wheel. However, the dealer and the pit inspector denied ever hearing the shout and refused to pay out. Howard went into the downstairs manager's office full of

Early Blackpool Years

rage to get a ruling but the manager backed his staff and refused the pay-out.

Everything seemed to die down until the doors to the gaming floor were flung open, and like a raging bull, Howard charged onto the gaming floor. Jumping on the roulette tables he proceeded to swing on the heavy chandeliers over the tables. From this he attacked the nearby blackjack tables, tipping them up, sending cards, chips and people scattering in all directions. His next victim was the roulette table itself. Now, Howard Plant was a very strong, beefy man but a roulette table is very heavy and it proved too much for the enraged Howard. He managed to get it to shoulder height but could not tip it over, he did however manage to fling the chips in each and every direction.

By this time people had cleared the gaming floor and were cowering in the restaurant and bar area of the casino. Howard was beginning to run out of steam by now, but continued to run round the gaming floor shouting obscenities directed mainly at the manager and staff.

Eventually people calmed him down and in due course the police came, but Howard was not charged with anything just banned for two years. They eventually let him back in, mainly I suspect because of the money he contributed to the casino through his gambling and private poker nights he ran in the casino, for which he paid the casino a table fee.

Edwina Stocker a.k.a. Rose Devine:

Rose breezed on to the poker scene quite unexpected; a woman of mystery, she just appeared one Saturday night and started playing. No one knew her, or her previous poker experience. She must have either played somewhere before, or studied the game, as while not a great player, she was obviously not a novice. Possibly in her late 40s, attractive in a mature way, short cropped black hair with ruby red lipstick and she always wore a leather cat suit, with thongs hanging from the sleeves and legs, all topped off with leather boots and a Homburg type hat. She called herself Rose Devine and spoke with a very upper class English accent. It later transpired that she was an actress, a thespian who owned, produced and acted in her own theatre company "Murder Mysteries", which operated around the North West in smaller theatres and other venues. Over time she became accepted in the poker fraternity around the Blackpool area.

Rose and I went to Vegas together. It was at a time when my personal life was in some disarray, and my second wife and I had just parted for a while. I had tickets for a week in Vegas for myself, my wife and her son, so not wanting to lose the cost of two tickets, I sold one to little Bill a poker friend from Manchester and the other to Rose. We would have to share a room of course at the Stratosphere, but no 'hanky panky', just two friends in Vegas for a week playing poker. It was at this time that I discovered Rose's real name of Edwina Stocker - I glimpsed it on her passport whilst going through Manchester airport. I kept it a secret, she just did not seem to be an Edwina.

All went well until we walked into the Stratosphere casino in Vegas, and Rose decided that she wanted her own room. Well, the cost of the pre-booked room was a very cheap $24 per night, (the rate I had paid) but the walk

Early Blackpool Years

in of the street cost (to Rose) would be $84 per night. Rose put on her very best upper crust accent, flung her arms around in true thespian manner and demanded to see the manager regarding this exorbitant difference in room rate. The duty manager duly appeared, but would have none of it - like all Vegas casino personal, he had seen it all before - so Rose had to cough up the higher rate.

We had a good weeks poker, and the American players at Binions, the Sahara and other card rooms fell in love with her. I think over the course of the week she lost a lot of money, but made lots of friends - it was a good trip.

After that I ran a home game for Rose, Thursday night and Sunday afternoon. It went well for a couple of years, but then came to a dramatic halt when Rose was arrested by the police and carted off to the local police station in a large black police van. She rang me in desperation after her release and we met in a cafe in Blackpool. Unknown to all, whilst acting and producing she was also claiming social benefits plus a big four wheel drive disability car, plus other financial assistance through having a bad back and unable to walk more than a hundred yards.

Rose's daughter had split from her boyfriend, and the boyfriend in a fit of revenge videoed Rose prancing and dancing on stage and sent the video to the Social Security. They had arrived at her door with the police and a search warrant and confiscated all her paper work, computer, bank statements etc; - and the rest is history.

Rose was eventually charged and received a fine and a suspended sentence. The last I heard of her was that she had returned to Cambridge to live with her mother. I hope she is ok.

Chapter 2

 Early Vegas Years:

The poker boom in was in its infancy when I first went to Las Vegas to witness the World Series of Poker, but most of the casinos had realised the potential of poker rooms on, or separate from the casino floor.

These years of the so called poker boom was a double edged sword to amateurs and relative new comers such as myself. This growth of the game was predominately fuelled by the televising of poker games and the development of the internet which allowed people to participate in a game of poker with other players from all over the world. In those early days of internet poker I played a lot on a site that no longer exists - 'Paradise Poker'. Evidence of how this initial interest has grown into a billion dollar industry can be seen in that one of the foremost sites 'Poker Stars' is now part of the 'Stars Group' that is listed on the New York Stock Exchange.

This expansion to the masses was good for the game but of course it allowed players to play uncontrolled and undoubtedly led to gambling problems and debt. It was also deficient in teaching the players the rules, etiquette and other important elements that go along with playing live poker. In those early years many online players would come into the casino to play live poker, and find a completely different game to the one they played in their lounge or bedroom - and on many, many occasions they had to be 're educated' by other players or the dealers.

The televising of poker also created a problem for new poker players. In a televised game of poker many of the boring and mundane hands are cut out of the final TV presentation, so the viewer does not get a true reflection of the game. Most of the hands presented are exciting hands that show lots of action and lots of bluffing. The new player then tries to emulate the professionals on the TV and bring these things into their game. A session of poker whether it be tournament or cash game play is nothing like this and adhere to the advice given throughout this book. If you want to learn the game, watch, read and perhaps play for small stakes online - but it is important that at an early stage in this process you go to a well run and professional game in a casino.

To illustrate this false exciting perception given by televised poker tournaments I quote this by one of the leading poker players Tom McEvoy in *'Poker & Pop Culture'* by Martin Harris:

'No-limit Hold'em: Hours of boredom followed by moments of sheer terror'.

In these early days of online and TV poker many of my friends from the early years made a reasonable living from playing poker online on what was termed 'rake back' sites. I know a few friends who gave up their regular jobs to concentrate on these online games. It worked like this: In the cash games, every time you were involved in a pot you got a percentage of the pot total, whether you won the pot or not. In theory, all you had to do over the day or week, was not to lose and if you broke even + the rake back you would be in profit. In effect it meant that you would have to play around 8 hours per day, sometimes on more than one table and not take too many chances.

I already had a good job in the Prison Service so was not interested in these sites. The few friends that were involved in these games made anything from £200 - £500 per week, but it was a hard, mundane way to make a living and did not last very long. I don't think these online sites exist anymore.

For the first ten years or so of my visits to Vegas I usually stayed Downtown and by my second or third trip practically all the casinos Downtown had vibrant poker rooms. The well established rooms of the Horseshoe, Golden Nugget and Plaza had been extended and the games available not only included the developing popular Texas Hold'em but also Seven Card Stud and Omaha. The Plaza also had a separate room just off the main poker area for Pai Gow.

Even the smaller casinos such as the Vegas Club, the Fremont, Fitzgeralds (now The D) and one of the earliest Vegas casinos, the El Cortez had small areas roped off for two or three tables of limit Texas Hold'em. The games available in these small casinos at this time was confined to $3 - $6 or $2 - $4 limit cash games. To the poker disadvantaged reader this means that the bets were limited to those particular amounts, or multiples of those amounts after the flop (first three cards dealt). None of these smaller rooms had tournaments available at this time. At this time the small stakes games of $2 - $4 or $3 - $6 available in the Downtown casinos outnumbers the now popular No Limit games where the amount of money a player can put into the pot at any stage of the hand is unlimited.

These small stake games were a godsend to beginners like myself, and it was by playing in these games that I learned the essentials of cash game play. One of the downsides of these games was that due to the increasing popularity of poker in Vegas at the time most of the higher end card rooms had taken the best dealers. Unlike the UK the poker dealers, the dealers in the USA only deal poker and not any of the other casino floor games and this makes them very proficient and knowledgeable in the game.

A bad or inexperienced dealer can make or break the pleasure of an eagerly anticipated session of poker. After playing in rooms at the Horseshoe or the Plaza, and then moving to Fitzgeralds it was most noticeable, and after many disputes between the players, the dealers and the card room manager at Fitzgeralds I actually stopped playing poker there. I had come to Vegas to enjoy my poker, win or lose, and did not want to sit through the endless delays whilst the dealers and the inexperienced card room manager came to (often wrongly) decisions on table disputes.

For a beginner like me, who at that time had only played in the Blackpool Saturday night £30 tournament sitting down in Las Vegas was mesmerizing - just to sit in Binion's Horseshoe and play in the same poker room as the greats I had only read about - and to think:

"Maybe Johnny Moss had played at this table; maybe Stu Unger had sat in this seat; maybe Tony Holden had sat riffling these chips whilst taking notes for 'Big Deal".
was spellbinding. Of course later on I was to see all the above in real life, but for that moment I was content just to be in the same arena as their memories.

These games also gave me confidence; confidence to try anything within my financial range; the confidence to recognise that in poker you need the desire to test yourself against better players, because that is the only way you are going to progress in the game. In her article on Psychology and Poker, Barbara Connors writes:

'Make no mistake, confidence is essential. You can't be a winning poker player without it. To withstand the brutal swings you must have faith in yourself'.

Along with this confidence comes the self-knowledge about your own ability. Playing against a better grade of player in poker invariably means higher stakes games, it is not like other sports, it will cost you money to learn and improve and your mistakes can be demoralising and sometimes lead to financial ruin - self confidence coupled with the awareness of your own limits is paramount. As Connors goes on to note:

'At the poker table, the ability to be uncompromisingly honest with yourself is worth its weight in gold'.

Early Vegas Years

In the same article Connors cites the *'serenity prayer'* as an example for poker players to follow when sitting down to play:

*'Grant me the serenity to accept the things I cannot change,
courage to change the things I can,
and the wisdom to know the difference'.*

Perhaps it is a good starting point.

One of the most upsetting memories of my early playing days at Blackpool which helped me in these early Vegas days was in regard to one of the other essentials of playing poker - that of discipline. I still remember with horror after all these years one night when I lost much more money than I could afford too. I went into the gents toilets at the end of the game and was physically sick. I can still recall after all these years the feeling of guilt and remorse of that night and the empty burning feeling in the pit of my stomach. The feeling that I would have to go home and lie to my wife about losing money that we had both worked hard for was terrifying. She invariably would ask me next day: *"How did it go last night?"* - I knew with the best intentions in the world that I could not tell her about the loss. It never happened again.

I have never been a addicted gambler but that night gave me a minute insight as to how a compulsive gambler must feel after losing money that they cannot afford. Although the money lost that night was not life savings, there are many documented occasions when compulsive gamblers have lost their houses, families, jobs etc; through chasing huge losses - I feel for them.

If I think back over my poker years this was perhaps the most singular lesson I learned from my early playing days - it taught me discipline, it taught me to know when to stop and cut my losses, it taught about going on tilt, it taught me never to sit down in a cash game without having a ceiling on the amount of money you are prepared to lose.

Early Vegas Years

This knowledge about your own level of skill and the ability to be honest with yourself in a place like Las Vegas is essential.

This recognition of 'stop losses' is not confined to low or medium stakes poker players. Former semi-professional soccer player Sam Trickett is now a UK high stakes poker player with some $20,849,721 in live poker earnings as of February 2019. He finished second to Antonio Esfandiari in the first Big One for One Drop at the World Series of Poker in 2012 winning $10 million in the process. In an interview for the Daily Star in 2018 Trickett said:

'The most I've won in a day is about £7.6 million/$9.9 million. I've lost £1 million/$1.3 million in a day a few times. If I thought I was going to lose more than that I'd feel uneasy. So, when that happens I tend to quit so I don't lose more'.

It is comforting for a small stakes player that even the most illustrious of poker professionals have the same instincts regarding their own particular level of losses.

I still remember the first poker hand I ever won in Las Vegas. It was in a $3 - $6 game in the above mentioned Fremont card room Downtown; a small card room that no longer exists and the winning hand was an Ace high club flush. I had hit the flush on the flop, and flat called it all the way down to the river card. I remember it was a small pot, and the lady sitting to my left who had donated most to the pot said: *"Well played, good hand",* little did she know that it was my inexperience that had led to me flat calling and not trying to build the pot by disguised actions, not good play. However, the size of the pot did not concern me, it was my first sit down in Vegas, it was my first win against regular Vegas poker players, and I was euphoric. I could not have been happier if I had won the World Series (well, perhaps not).

In those early days, I played a lot of poker in Circus Circus and would at times wander around the casino and venture into the Casino Gift Shop. It was hard to imagine that this innocuous looking shop full of Las Vegas tat was actually the front for one of the mafia's most feared hit men. Tony Spilotro was a Chicago mob enforcer, nicknamed 'Tony the Ant' who was sent out to Las Vegas in the late 1950s to oversee the Chicago's Mob's interest in Las Vegas. He purchased the Gift Shop in Circus Circus for a reputed $70,000 with funds from the Teamsters Central States Pension fund. This shop became the front for Spilotro's loan sharking and bookie operations in Las Vegas.

He eventually sold the shop for a reputed $700,000 in 1972 when new Circus Circus owners decided that all concessions in the casino would be run by the owners of the casino. Spilotro was one of the most ruthless killers to operated in Las Vegas, and went on to establish and operate the famous 'hole in the wall' gang in Las Vegas. He was eventually, along with his brother, executed himself by the mafia for breaking strict mafia rules. Spilotro's reign of terror in Las Vegas and his death is portrayed by Joe Pesci in the film *'Casino'*. I often wondered whilst walking past the shop how many of the people casually browsing around knew the true history of the Gift Shop and its past owners.

Another of my regular poker haunts in these early years was the Stardust. This is another casino that had a heavy mafia influence. It was only a small card room with only five poker tables and catered mainly for the small stakes cash player. I have sat in the room for many hours ruminating on what had gone before. The Stardust had always been associated with the mob and its demised can be read in Steve Fischers *'When the Mob Ran Vegas'* in more detail.

The Stardust is the casino represented as the Tangiers in the film *'Casino'*. The casino manager at the Stardust for many years was Frank Rosenthal, also known as 'Lefty', and of course his friendship with Tony Spilotro (noted above) is well epitomized in the film. These real characters (not the actors) would have sat in that same Stardust coffee shop over the years as I did in the early nineties. I was plotting how to win at the $3 - $6 poker game - I suspect they would have been plotting on matters of higher financial stakes!

Another coincidence event in one of these early games at the Stardust was in a game involving a Scottish player. He was trying to give the impression of being an experienced knowledgeable poker player. In one hand he was staring at me for quite a while. I had not spoken during the game so he did not know I was British:

"What's the problem?" I asked.

"Just trying to get a read on you" he answered.

"Look pal", I said, *"We are playing a $3 - $ 6 low stakes game here. If you want that type of action go down the road to the World Series at Binions".*

He blushed noticeably and realised how silly he looked trying high stakes ploys in a $3 -$6 game.

A few years later the same man walked into the poker room at the Grosvenor casino at Blackpool one Saturday night. He was down from Glasgow for a week's holiday and to player poker. He recognised me straight away and we had a laugh about Vegas. He turned out to be a really nice guy explaining that it had been his first visit to Vegas and was trying to impress.

On my return from my many trips to Vegas over the years, the first thing friends and family will say: *"Oooh did you win".* I look at these questioners, asking in their naivety and try to explain, without much success to these non gamblers - that if you come back from two weeks gambling in Vegas breaking even, then you have won. They don't seem to grasp it.

The total take of the casinos per year just on the Las Vegas strip alone is somewhere around $27 billion per year, that is a daily average of around $650,000 a day per casino. Some of the larger and more expensive casinos take more; e.g, the Wynn needs to make at least $1 million

Early Vegas Years

dollars per day just to survive and pay off the bank loan + interest taken out in its creation - and it does! They don't manage to do this if people win or break even. It is also hard to explain to people why gamblers enjoy the experience of Vegas win or lose. You know where you stand with the city and its occupants, they make no bones about it - yes, we will comp you, be nice to you, have a nice day etc,. etc., but we are here to take your money, in any which way we can. We will do it at every opportunity, at every turn, squeeze you until you squeak, and surrender every last drop of sweat and greenback to our coffers. I love it!

In his book *'Ghosts at the Table'* Des Wilson quotes a reference from the Los Angeles Times to gambling and poker establishments of the late 19th century in the American West:

'These saloons, gambling joints and Honky Tonks had one main purpose - the taking of the cattleman's money as quickly as possible'.

So then, apart from the clientele nothing has changed!

Apart from the above desire to take your money, Las Vegas has changed dramatically over the 30 years that I have had the pleasure of its company. Whether or not that is for the better very much depends on your personal point of view. No more is it more evident from the perspective of the gambler, low stakes grinder, fun loving amateur or the high roller ('whales' - to use Vegas casino jargon). It makes no difference; the gambler's world has changed spectacularly for the worse. For years every poker room had free food on the go for most of the day, coffee and donuts in the morning, pizza and fries during the day and free vouchers for the casino buffet in the evening. If you had one of these gambler's vouchers, then you went to the front of the buffet queue. Not really any big deal, but it made you feel important walking past the early evening line up.

Early Vegas Years

One of the comps (compliments) still in existence is the hotel room upgrade. The hotels in Las Vegas have you on record for an eternity and on the majority of occasions I have booked in at a hotel that I have frequented over the years I get a room upgrade. The casinos keep a record of everything; they can tell how many hours poker I have played in their card room, how many free meals I have had, how many times I have played a slot machine (on a slots ticket), which room I stayed in 5 years ago etc, etc. As a regular poker player I can get certain comps and these include: a couple of free nights, room rate reduction, upgrade on the room and waiver of the dreaded compulsory resort fee. In the great scheme of Vegas high rollers and gamblers these small concessions are not big deals, but they make you feel important.

To book a two week holiday in Vegas, I used to book through the card room manager, and get a special rate. It usually went something like this:

"Hi Jerry, its Mike Connah from England, can you book me in for two weeks?".

"Sure Mike, when you coming?".

"1st May, Jerry, can I get poker rates and overseas rate, and do I have to play so many hours to get them?".

"Sure Mike, don't worry about the hours, I know you are a poker player, just show your face every now and then in the card room".

"Cheers Jerry, see you in May".

That is all it took to get a discounted room in Jackie Gaughan's Plaza downtown on Fremont Street for $24 per night. Unfortunately, after a few years of this Jerry Rowell the card room manager and some of the dealers in the Plaza card room got the sack for creaming off money from the card room take! That was the end of my cheap Plaza stays and probably the end of Jerry ever working again in Vegas.

I was surprised that this was all the punishment they received for this scam. Jackie Gaughan was well

Early Vegas Years

connected with certain business gentlemen of Italian descent. He had bought one of his other casinos, the El Cortez from an associate of Bugsy Siegel and although Benjamin Siegel was long gone by then one of his bodyguards, Fat Irish Green still lived free of charge in the El Cortez. Jackie Gaughan had lots of contacts; Jerry and the other dealers were very lucky!

The overseas rate for poker players came to an end soon after this period as the 'Benidorm clique' decided to descend on Vegas instead of the Costa del Sol. One of the things I dread in Vegas is hearing an English accent, especially at the poker table where I cannot escape. Experience has shown me that ninety percent of the time they are going to embarrass me. The package holiday firms and their cheap flights have a lot to answer for!

Other freebies for the gamblers included free bus trips to Laughlin, which is a scenic two hour drive across the desert. The air-conditioned bus would pick you up from your hotel, take you to Laughlin and bring you back around 5pm. It included some free gambling vouchers and vouchers for a lunch time buffet at the Colorado Bell Casino on the Colorado River. All this was free, and paid for by the casinos in Lauchlin to get gamblers down from Vegas for the day, the only cost was a $5 tip for the driver, who would give a running commentary about the history of the desert region and its mines.

All the Las Vegas casino reception areas had free 'see Vegas' magazines. These magazines contained hundreds of vouchers for free slots play, hot dog lunches, Vegas key rings and ornaments, free beers at various bars, discounts for the Las Vegas shows etc. All gone now in the interest of corporate profit!

Early Vegas Years

Vegas Trivia:

The name Las Vegas means 'The Meadows' in Spanish.

When first built The MGM grand has 5,000 rooms. When it was full, which it often was, it was at the time the 5th largest city in Nevada.

The steel wiring in the concrete tower of the Stratosphere if stretched out would be 200 miles long.

The usual summer temperature in Vegas is 110f - 112f. They have rest stations along the strip, with large fans spraying cool water for pedestrians.

There are 39 million visitors per year to Vegas.

It is a crime to take off your shirt on the Las Vegas strip.

It is estimated that more than a thousand people live under the city in the flood tunnels of Las Vegas. Many of the drain dwellers have made subterranean homes in the 200 miles of tunnelling.

Part II: Las Vegas

Sin City
I was there when
Only in Vegas
The Dark Side of Vegas
Vegas Casinos
Vegas Trivia
Getting Married in Vegas

Chapter 1

Sin City:

I have travelled extensively in my life and seen many parts of the world, from the Northern wastes of the Arctic circle to the jungles of Borneo; from bathing on the beaches of Hawaii and Barbados to driving through the Rocky Mountains of Canada; from sailing inside the Great Barrier Reef to transiting the Panama and Suez canals.

But none of these global travels can compare with the thrill of flying into McCarren International airport in Vegas on a hot day in July. The feeling of anticipation and excitement begins at 35,000 feet and some 250 miles North West of Vegas as the pilot advises passengers that they can see the Grand Canyon through the right hand side windows. Of course, I am not interested in a big hole in the ground because a little bell has just gone off in my head and I my brain is beginning to work again after the monotony of the ten hour flight from the UK. These feelings intensify as a few minutes later you pass over Lake Mead and the Hoover Dam, the 'seat belt' sign is illuminated and the pilot starts his descent path. This anticipation is like an injected drug coursing through the gamblers veins.

This 'anticipation' narcotic is no more expressively described than by Marvin Karlins in his book *'A Chip and a Prayer'*. Karlins taught Singapore Airline pilots at Changi Airport in Singapore. He describes how he would land in Los Angeles after a seventeen hour flight from Singapore and would then drive 4 hours from LA to Vegas instead of taking a 1 hour flight, using the extra time taken just to enjoy the anticipation of the gambling that was to come. As he says in the book: *'Unlike gambling, anticipation is free'.*

As the plane descends over the tops of the mountains surrounding Vegas, you can see the strip and the associate casinos shimmering in the desert heat below. A wondrous, exhilarating sight for the occasional first time visitor, but for the gambler it is the reason to live, the crock of gold at the end of the rainbow, the glimpse of heaven.

The long dreary nightmare 10 hour flight from UK seems to dissipate into oblivion and you realise that reality is behind you and you will soon be in the land of make believe.

Then, as if to re-enforce the perception that reality has been left behind the visitor is greeted in typical Las Vegas style enticing the new arrivals to gamble with cut price hotel rates, offering shows, girls - persuasive voices shout out from hidden speakers: *"Hello there, welcome to Las Vegas - take time to play - the temperature outside is.............."* . The weary traveller is then assailed by the sounds of clinking slot machines immediately you exit the 'yes sir'; 'no sir', American process of immigration. After my first few years of visiting I realized that the stern officious looking bureaucrats are not without humour and do in fact to have a heart. I was pleasantly surprised one year when I tried to push my luck, and to the compulsory question:

"What is the nature of your visit to the USA today sir?".
I looked him in the eye and said:
"To donate to the USA tax revenues sir".

His face melted and he smiled, and then quite oblivious of the hundreds behind me who had just embarked from the A330, he started a friendly conversation about the time he had spent in the US Air Force based in Norfolk in the UK. He had noticed my tattoos and quite rightly assumed I had been in the armed forces, or Military as the Americans refer to it.

Sin City

After immigration the passengers then enter the horror of the baggage carousel hall where immediately the first time visitor is hit by the understanding of Vegas fantasy land - never before have they seen a maze of slot machines, one armed bandits, gaming machines and free drink, food, excursions etc on the way to the carousel area - welcome to La La land. I try to get through immigration quickly, hit the baggage carousel first, smile and think - I'm home.

In those early days after getting over the shock of the desert heat that hits you as you walk out of the air-conditioned airport, I would catch the Bell's transfer bus - just $5 wherever you go; the bus stops at all the casinos required by the passengers. Not only was it much cheaper than the taxi but much more fun. You swop stories with your fellow passengers about their journey, where they come from, what are they going to gamble on, how much have they paid for the hotel room etc, etc. "*I got a room at so and so with 15 bucks of the room rate, and a free breakfast*" - but of course you know that the rather large lady from Phoenix who educated the other passengers with her good fortune would probably stick twice that amount into a gaming machine within the first hour in the casino. Living and eating is cheap in Las Vegas - it is the playing that is expensive.

I have drunk pints of Green Raw Scrumpy in the cider pubs of Plymouth; sickly Uozo in Gribraltar; Tiger beer and Singapore Slings at Raffles in Singapore; Sake in Japanese bars in San Francisco and White Rum in Bridgetown, Barbados.

But none of the above can match up to sitting down with a cold bottle of Budweiser at a poker table in Las Vegas. Then when you sit down for your first hand of poker in the card room, the familiar sounds of a Vegas poker room hit you: *"Seat empty table five"* (shouted by dealer); *"Cocktails, any drinks here?"* (shouted by cocktail waitress); *"Will all tournament players take their seats"* (intercom card room manager); - then you really know you are home!

The above Vegas events have their own very different and very unique feelings, the first knowing that you are just a few minutes and a few thousand feet from walking into the heady, giddy atmosphere of a hectic Vegas casino with its unconventional but exclusive occupants, a unique world which you are soon to be a part of. The other is the calming, relaxing feelings of sitting down with strangers, but like minded people from all different parts of the world and backgrounds. People from Germany, USA, Japan, Canada who will all speak the common vocabulary of poker - the flop, big slick, the river, suited connectors etc, etc. It feels like being part of a big unique international family where money or social class is irrelevant.

Over the years many people have asked me: *"What is Las Vegas like?"*.

It is perhaps easier to describe what Las Vegas is not like; it is not like as portrayed on many films or documentaries. For instance, there was a TV documentary called *'The Strip'* about the Las Vegas police department and how they police Las Vegas Boulevard South (the Strip). Every week the viewer would see multiple arrests and warnings issued to mainly drunk or drug induced characters, some amusing and entertaining, some more serious. I have been going to Las Vegas for over thirty years, and never seen any trouble either through drink or drugs. I am not suggesting that these issues do not occur in Las Vegas, they do just the same as other large cities throughout the world. The most serious offence I have seen on the Strip is some teenager skateboarders being ordered and chased from the front of New York, New York's plaza by their own security staff! Not quite a Federal offence!

So, what is Las Vegas like?

The first thing to mention is that it is safe, especially in the casinos where they have their own security. I have never seen a police officer on foot on the strip. What is not commonly known is that the casinos own the pavement in front of their particular casino and so their own security personnel police those areas. Providing you stick to the main tourist areas, it is as save as any other big city. It is not just casinos and strip clubs; it has a tremendous amount to offer other than gambling: weather, shopping, shows, sightseeing. Everything is open twenty four hours a day - casinos, bars, restaurants are usually accessible at all hours.

It is a real city with a University, three big hospitals, churches for every denomination and nearly three million residents many of whom have never gambled in their lives. I remember once going to the Trinity Methodist Church on West Charleston Boulevard one Sunday morning many years ago. I had taken a taxi to get there, but a couple I met at the after service coffee and biscuits offered to take me back to the hotel. As we drove onto the North end of the strip, the woman turned to her husband, and said:

"Oh, look at that new casino going up there".

"First time you have seen it?" I asked.

"Oh yes", she said, "It must be nearly four years since I was on the strip".

Las Vegas residents live normal lives, and if they are not involved in the tourist industry or don't gamble, then there is no need to go on the strip. Vegas is a big place full of 'normal' people.

In fact it is in the residential area that Las Vegas is expanding and not the casino and entertainment area. The current population (2020) is 662,2000 making it the 26th largest city in the US with approximately 5,000 people moving into Clark County every month (United States Census Bureau).

Over the course of my visits to Vegas I have spoke to many who live and work in the city and on most occasions the first introduction to this discourse is my question: *"Do you come from Vegas?".* Over those years I believe I have only found a handful of people who were actually born and raised in Vegas or the surrounding suburbs - or in fact in the state of Nevada itself. It appears that no one is ever born here, and if they do, they get out at the earliest opportunity! Everyone seems to come from somewhere else and it is almost impossible to find a native 'Vegaser'.

This of course adds to the attraction of the place as a transient city, this adds to the interest the mystery of the place and to the vast number of people who have stories to tell - what did they do before Vegas? - what drove them to live here? - are they hiding something? Why?, why? I have often thought whilst people watching on the strip or my usual casino haunts that a book could be filled with these stories and I love to hear these personal accounts from the friends I have made over the years. So why do these people move to Vegas?

I think it probably falls into the two obvious categories: the mentioned easy and cheap retirement living and to work in the entertainment or gambling industry in some way. There are some other reasons that my Vegas friends and others I have accounted give; the weather is another popular reason for moving to Vegas - you don't have to buy winter clothes, you can exist with just a T shirt and shorts for 10 months of the year. As mentioned, the local 'Vegasers' rarely spend time in the sun, and with all cars, houses and establishments having air conditioning, the blistering desert heat is liveable.

Property is cheap in Las Vegas compared to other US cities of a similar size. The cost of living plus a rented property is estimated at: in New York $7,000 per month, in San Francisco of $8,100 in Las Vegas $3,800 per month (Las Vegas Real Estate). Las Vegas also has a disproportionate number of retirement complexes compared with other large cities, making it easier for retirees to sell up and move into luxury accommodation without having to buy another home. If the retiree wants to purchase another home then the majority of new developments are in gated communities, where the home owner can feel safe. All the above plus the opportunities of part time work in the entertainment or gaming industry makes it an attractive incentive for the retiree or semi retiree to move to Vegas.

Las Vegas also has other advantageous that possibly apply more to the younger generation. Although the suburbs have pretty standard hours, having the strip only 15-20 minutes away from most places in the city means you can find something to do 24 hours a day. Opportunities abound in Vegas for jobs in the hospitality industry, from hotels, casinos and restaurants to bars, clubs and performance venues. But for those with a desire work in other areas there is also a strong realm of business which offers a multitude of employment options for perhaps the more educated mind. The University of Nevada (UNLV) is a research university with a 332-acre main campus and is in the middle tier of the US nationwide Overall Best College rankings (ww.collegefactual.com). The University is in a prime location situated just 1.5 miles off the Strip. This close location to the tourist centre of Las Vegas makes it ideal for any student wishing to supplement their University income with part time employment. It is no surprise the University's College of Hospitality's Administration programme is ranked number 2 in the world (QS World University Rankings).

Despite a perception that Las Vegas is expensive, living in Vegas is relatively inexpensive compared to other major US cities. Taxes, petrol, food, entertainment etc is cheaper with plenty of other perks available to the residents of this isolated city in the middle of the Mohave Desert. The state of Nevada has zero local tax as the revenue from gaming and the casinos taxes benefits the local residents. It is little wonder that so many US citizens choose Vegas as their number one retirement destination, as their Social security income and retirement account income are not taxed.

Sin City

Although there had been settlers in the region previously, mostly Mormons sent by Brigham Young in 1855, Las Vegas was not officially recognised until May 1905. It grew out of a land auction held by the San Pedro, Los Angeles & Salt Lake Railroad Company and later flourished when the state of Nevada legalized gambling in 1931. It further grew when the federal government decided to build the Hoover Dam in nearby Boulder City and Las Vegas was the nearest town of any significance in which the workers could relax, drink and gamble their money away.

Las Vegas is located in the Mojave, one of the great deserts of North America and many tourists and gamblers do not realize the beauty of the desert and mountains surrounding Las Vegas. The Las Vegas valley was once billions of years ago an inland sea with surrounding mountains with a total of 52 peaks in all the mountain ranges, and non being more majestic than Mount Charleston at 11.916 feet the highest peak in the mountain ranges surrounding Las Vegas (In Spanish Las Vegas means 'The Meadows - Marshy Place').

In my early visits to Vegas I would always drive out along East Charleston Boulevard, through Red Rock Canyon and drive slowly to the peak, looking in admiration at this natural beauty and relaxing peace just 35 miles North West of the bustling, noisy cacophony of Vegas. Passing the Joshua trees that only grow in this part of the USA and at a height between 1,300 and 5,900 feet elevation you can feel the air cooling around you until you reach the top and realise there is snow at various depths around you. It seems bizarre that you are in 100 degrees of stifling early Summer heat and just a 20 minutes' drive later you are standing in 7 inches of snow.

It is worth the journey across the desert alone just to see the wild burros grazing at the road side and to see the Joshua trees, which suddenly appear at a certain height, and then disappear just as quickly a few thousand metres higher. The Joshua tree was named by the original Mormon settlers because of its similarity to the biblical Joshua reaching upwards, arms outstretched to heaven. The native American Southern Paiute name for Mount Charleston is 'Nuvagantu', literally 'where snow sits'.

Red Rock Canyon is another scenic treasure of the Las Vegas Valley. Only a short drive away from the Strip it is another area I visited year after year in those early days when I had a car. The area obviously gets its name from the large red rock formations in its peaks, the highest of which is known as the Keystone Thrust. The highest peak in these formations is the Madre Mountain at some 8,154 feet. If you venture into these canyons there is a variety of plant life that feeds of the canyon springs and there are still some petroglyphs which were carved by the Southern Paiute Indians hundreds of years ago.

There are many other natural beauty spots within driving distance of Las Vegas that unfortunately the tourist who just come to party and gamble do not see. When I hear people say: *"We went to Las Vegas for a week"* I listen with a tinge of sadness as I know they will not have had time to visit these wonderful natural backdrops. Apart from the almost compulsory trip to the Grand Canyon they do not venture outside Vegas.

I must admit at this point however to my hypocrisy, as I have never visited the Grand Canyon - my defence is that it is too far away and whichever way you travel, it will take up a full day. I often compound my hypocrisy by saying to inquirers: *"Why do I want to travel 5,000 miles and waste a day's poker to see a hole in the ground?"* - I will go one day (I think).

Other areas of outstanding beauty around Las Vegas that I have visited are Valley of Fire State Park; The Hoover Dam; Lake Mead and some of the now derelict silver mines. All of them well worth wasting a day's poker for (I think).

Sin City

Las Vegas is of course synonymous with Benjamin 'Bugsy' Siegel who was sent by his Chicago Mafia bosses to set up an illegal racing wire with the outfits Trans-America Wire Service. It was during this time that Siegel used the mob's money to build the Flamingo hotel in the desert, just outside Las Vegas in Clark County. He named the hotel after his pet name for his mistress Virginia Hill. The Flamingo defied all the odds of a casino and lost money in its first few years with the Mafia bosses back in Chicago believing Siegel was 'skimming' money from the profits. Siegel was eventually shot on June 20th 1947.

The casino was then taken over by Moe Sedway and Gus Greenbaun from the nearby El Cortez Hotel. The casino flourished, more and more casinos were built - and the rest is history. The Flamingo is still there, complete with real live flamingos in its nature gardens. In the middle of the casino is a large round bar, aptly named 'Bugsy's Bar' - I make it a must on my trips to Vegas to have a least one visit, sit at the bar and raise a beer to 'Bugsy'. There used to be a rose garden aptly named 'Bugsy's Rose Garden' in memory of the founder, but it is no more, it was dug up when they built the new tower which increased the hotel capacity to 3,500 rooms.

Mobsters or 'the boys' as they were always referred to in Las Vegas were mostly in control of Vegas in the early years but their decline in Vegas started in the late sixties when the Corporate Gaming Act was introduced in Nevada which included a more in depth check on the casinos operators. It allowed rich business men such as Kirk Kerkorian (the Flamingo) and Howard Hughes (the Desert Inn) to move in and fill the gap left by 'the boys'. The early days of the old Mafioso was coming to an end and the days of Siegel, Lansky, Costello and Moe Dalitz were numbered, and casinos like the Dunes, the Stardust, the Riviera and the Tropicana fell into the hands of big business led corporations such as Caesars Entertainments,

Sin City

MGM resort properties, Wynn Resorts, Boyd Gaming and a multitude of other smaller concerns.

For those who are interested in such things - most of the Mafia involvement in Las Vegas was from the Chicago and to a lesser extent the Kansas City 'boys'. There was a brokered agreement between the major US families, that the New York families would take Atlantic City and the Chicago families take Nevada.

Some would say this is a bad thing. I'm not going to collude with this thinking, suffice to say that low hotel prices and the many 'freebies' were consistently the same over the era of Vegas mob control. The Mafia would take their illegal cut of the profits out of the casino count room, and everyone was happy except the tax man. The mob was also tolerated - and to some - liked by the local Las Vegas residents as they kept all the other criminals out of the city thus keeping a sense of residential security. It could be said that the era of organized crime in Vegas finished with the imprisonment of Don Angelina, known as 'The Wizard of the Odds', the last head of the mob in Las Vegas in 1993.

Now the big corporations want to make increased profits year on year making price rises and the cutting of free complimentary items inevitable. So, from the gamblers financial point of view it was much better with the mob in control, although maybe not from an ethical or law abiding viewpoint, or from the American tax payers view.

Mobsters do still have a hand in a lot of the casino related activities in Las Vegas. Some of the smaller casinos still have mob backed organisations managing the casinos, and they are still active in other criminal behaviours such as loan sharking, extortion and robberies. However, it is true to say that the Mafia and other criminal organisations do not have the foot hold they once did in the early days of Vegas.

Sin City

One of the events that was not in operation in the original Flamingo is the 'pool party'. The Flamingo is no exception in holding these seemingly twenty four hour parties, which have become very popular in Las Vegas over the last five years or so. As an aged, sedentary poker player I have of course never been immersed in these wild, boisterous revelries, but I have witnessed them from a prudent and cautious distance. What surprised me was the security on show at the Flamingo pool to actually enter the merriment. I counted eleven yellow shirted security personnel, complete with radios, guns and all the paraphernalia of an FBI agent. There were two separate stations that the party goers had to check through; a personal search and then a bag search. In fact, it appeared harder to get into the Flamingo's pool party than to proceed through immigration at Manchester Airport! Again, everyone was going through this search procedure with good humour and high spirits. I watched for about ten minutes, then the noise finally got to me and I left for the relative serenity of the poker room.

The place has a kind of romanticism that grips visitors, gamblers or not. The people who come to Vegas either to gamble or just to soak up the atmosphere of the place because it was on their 'bucket list' is a diverse assortment of individuals from all walks of life. The middle class American retirees from the Northern States in their garish jump suits and pale sun deprived skin usually with the biggest bottoms on the earth, the young fund managers from California in their trendy Cargo shorts with tanned legs and sporty demeanour; the Asian and Mexican families trundling around with pushchairs gawping at the opulence around them, and the beer bellied, tattooed, Big Mac bikers from Texas and the Southern States. During my visits I have met them all, and in the main I have found them enjoyable to talk to, to swop stories with and genuinely good people. The Americans are lovely, friendly people underneath their sometimes brash and loud exterior and over the years I have become to enjoy their company.

However, I have found that one thing is common, in that the majority have very little knowledge of the world outside America. Whether this is because of the educational system, or the media's focus on the USA, I do not know, but during my visits and conversations I have had some bizarre questions asked of me. Statements and questions such as:

"Do they have colour television in England?".
"But, the Queen is not a real person, is she?".
"Is Scotland in England?".

Another feature of UK life that I have learned the Americans cannot understand is the NHS. I cannot remember how the conversation arrived at this point, but remember very well how it went. The conversation was between myself and two well dressed and obviously intelligent couples in the Excalibur Sports Book.

They just could not grasp how I could go to the doctor, be referred to a specialist, go into hospital and have treatment without cost. Or, how I could turn up at A & E and be admitted to the hospital and undergo expensive tests and receive treatment without cost.

Of course I explained to them that all my working life I had been paying something called National Insurance, and that is how I and my employers have actually contributed to my treatment, and that we do have private hospitals in the UK, so you could fund your costs privately.

"So", one of the ladies said, *"what if you don't work, do you get the same treatment?".*

"Yes" I said: *"Doesn't matter if you are a vagrant or a rich business man - the treatment is the same".*

They could just not grasp the concept of this.

"Well, what - let's say - you broke your leg and went to hospital A & E and got treated, how much would it cost?", one of the ladies asked.

"No idea, not got a clue", I said.

The conversation went on like this for quite a while, but they just could not understand the concept of a National Health Service. Medical Insurance is a very complicated business in the USA with differing private and government schemes and these people just could not understand how such a simple system could work.

Another rather strange example of this American characteristic I witnessed was whilst playing one day at Circus Circus. I got into conversation with an English player who like me was also ex Royal Navy. In one of the hands there was just this player and myself left in the hand and he won the hand. By the 'rules' I am not required to show my hand if I fold and capitulate, but one of the American players at the table demanded of the dealer that I show my hand. I did this just to keep the table happy and friendly but when I inquired of him why he had demanded this he said:

"Well, you both speak the same English lingo and might be playing together". I looked at him in amazement and said:

"Look, I have only just met the man, I have no idea who he is", and went on to explain that I came from the North of England and the gentleman lived on the South Coast.

"Well, yea" came the reply, *"But England is such a small place you probably know each other".*

There is no answer to this geographical ignorance, so I let the matter drop.

I met and played against the above mentioned ex Royal Navy player over the next few years (I have sadly forgot his name), and we chatted for many hours over the times we had spent in the 'Andrew'. He came to Vegas twice a year - April and September, and on the last occasion I saw him he gave me a bundle of letters and asked me to post them on my return to UK. I was a bit dubious about this at first, but he explained - over the years he had become familiar with a nice respectful Vegas divorcee, had been offered a job as the front man at a car dealership (they liked his UK accent) and had decided to marry the lady and stay. The letters were to his son and his family explaining the situation and his reasons. Unfortunately as mention elsewhere, the Circus Circus poker room shut down shortly after this, and I never saw him again. Hope it worked out for him.

Another example of the American people sometimes not being in tune with the rest of the world was a personal experience which I had with a friend who lives in Vegas. This friend is a practicing Christian like myself, and would frequently pick me up from the hotel and take me to her church. It appears that her church had decided to send a team to the immigration camps that had sprung up around Calais and other areas of Northern France hoping to bring some sort of relief, especially to the children in the camps. This of course was a wonderful Christian effort on the church's behalf especially as most of the team would be footing the bill themselves, and I do not want to degenerate their motives in any way.

After church we went for lunch where she broached the subject, asking me the best way to travel across UK with a view to getting the train from London to Paris (the flight was via Gatwick).

"Remember", she said *"We will have lots of luggage and bags of fluffy toys for the children"*.

I looked at her in amazement and said:

"R.A. - fluffy toys? - these people have no clothes, no belongings, are starving with no shelter and no medication - and you want to cart fluffy toys all the way from Vegas?".

I also tried to explain to her that the vast majority of people in UK - Christian and non Christians alike, whilst having the greatest sympathy for these poor souls did not want them coming to England. I also, warned her that large numbers in these camps were young single men and that they were economical migrants, and not asylum seekers. She just did not understand. I added that perhaps she and her church could spend the money and time better in helping the addicts and homeless in Vegas. I also added that if the church team did go (I think the flights and other travel arrangements had already been booked when she spoke to me) - it would be better for the children if she took warm clothing and maybe some chocolate for the children, and not fluffy toys.

Of course it was a wonderful well meaning mission, but the ignorance of the reality of the situation in Europe and these camps at that time of uncontrolled immigration was toxic - and in fact dangerous for them.

R.A. and her team went to Northern France and on my next visit to Vegas we talked briefly about it. She did admit that they were totally unprepared for what they witnessed. The vast majority of people they came into contact with were the above mentioned young men who wanted nothing to do with her Christianity or the kindness they were trying to give. She was disappointed, and I think that they finished up by helping in the mobile food kitchens that had been set up by other voluntary organisations.

I teach English Language for a living and I am a confessed language freak. So when I go to Vegas I like to play around with the language and I am always engrossed whilst there in analysing how much American English is moving away from what might be termed English.

Sometimes I find it very difficult to understand what the good people of America are saying, or the meaning they are trying to get across. Americans speak in a very metaphoric style of language which as a linguist I find fascinating. At the coffee counter: *"The cream **will be** at the end of the counter sir"*. What?, when? later today or tomorrow? And the intercom on the strip bus: *"Please have the correct amount of money, the driver does not **make** change"*. Well, no I suppose he does not have the time or the facilities to do this whilst driving.

One incident I remember vividly from many years ago was in the company of a young black guy on the Strip bus (The Deuce). I cannot remember how we got into conversation but we did - for some 20 minutes, and at the end of the journey I had no idea what he had been talking about! The only thing I could deduce was that it was something to do with his ex wife and access to his son.

On a more recent occasion a young sales girl in Harrahs' gift shop approached me to ask if she could be of any assistance. She then went into a long obviously rehearsed script for about 3 or 4 minutes - I never understood a word of it. English was obviously her first language but she spoke so fast it was impossible for me to grasp the message. She was a lovely, sweet young girl obviously trying to do her job - so I did not want to appear rude to her, but just had to say:

"Look, I'm terribly sorry but I just could not follow what you said, could you say again, but slower?".

She did, but I have to admit it was not much better.

One of the big attractions in Las Vegas are of course the shows. The history of the Vegas shows with Frank Sinatra's Rat Pack leading the way in the 1960's, followed by such greats of the entertainment world as: Judy Garland; Elvis Presley; Celion Dion; Barbara Streisand. Many of the theatres in the larger casinos are named after these long standing Vegas performers. The significance of the entertainment industry as a contributor to Las Vegas in both a financial and tourist perspective is that it has bought over countless years many non gamblers to the city. Although of course many of these tourists will (as noted later on) not want to come to Vegas without going home and telling family and friends that they gambled a little.

The popularity of these Vegas shows can be seen in a personal episode of mine and my first wife H. It was April and we wanted to book to see Celion Dion at Caesars Palace, on inquiring as to availability and cost, we were told that the cheapest seats were $100 - back in the Gods somewhere - and nothing was available until August!

I must admit to the reader that I am not a lover of Las Vegas shows. When people who know me are visiting Las Vegas for the first time they invariably ask about shows. My advice is to yes, see a show just for the experience but be prepared to pay top class prices for a top class show. There are lots of smaller shows, or matinees that are reasonably cheap, but if you want to see international headliners then you have to pay top rates. Another downside is that in some of the smaller casino theatres you cannot book a particular seat in a particular part of the theatre. All the seats are the same price and whether or not you get a good view depends on if, or how much, you tip the maitre d whilst being shown to your seat.

It has been my Vegas show experience that they do not change from year to year. I have personal experience of this whilst going to see one of Las Vegas' sons Lance Burton. Burton was one of the foremost magicians at the time, and possibly the best who used doves in his magic act. I went to see him perform at the Hacienda, a South Strip casino that no longer exists. During the performance he would sit on the front of the stage to talk to the audience for a few minutes talking about the last illusion he had performed. During this someone shouted out:

"How's it done?", to which Burton replied:

"If I told you that, I would need to kill you afterwards", to which the reply came back from the audience:

"Ok then - tell my wife".

Some years later after the Hacienda had been demolished Burton moved on to the Monte Carlo into a theatre named after him. I went to see him again foolishly thinking the show must have changed after all these years and a different location. It hadn't. Not only was the above incident recreated to the very word, but his supporting juggling act from the old Hacienda was in the Monte Carlo show doing exactly the same act. Just as a matter of note the Monte Carlo now belongs to the MGM corporation, and has been refurbished.

Burton still lives in Las Vegas and a couple of years ago I got into conversation with a magician who works part time in the Magic Shop in New York, New York. I got into the habit as I past the shop, if he was not busy of going in and talking to him about magic. On one occasion I related the above story to him, and he said:

"Look, I am a friend of Lance, and see him occasionally for coffee, how would you like to come along and talk magic?".

"Ok", I said, "next time I am passing and you are in, I will call in and we can set something up".

Regretfully, I never did - he was only part time in the shop, and my non poker time in Vegas is limited, so it never happened. I always think that if it did, would I have mentioned to Burton the above story? - I doubt it.

Apart from the shows Las Vegas has been the background or the set for many successful movies. Amongst them are: The Godfather; Oceans 11; Casino; Indecent Proposal and Honeymoon in Vegas. One of my furtive delights over the years when visiting Vegas has been to visit as many as these sets as I can. One of my addictions is to walk around the Bellagio where perhaps my favourite film Oceans 11 was made - search the staircase that Julie Roberts (Tess) walked down in the film; walk down the gaming floor aisle where Carl Reiner (Saul) walked down, sit in the restaurant where Andy Garcia (Terry) sat with Tess. One of my 'always without fail' events is to stand in the viewing bay overlooking the Bellagio Fountain display where the gang stood after the robbery and peeled away slowly, one by one. Addicted! - not me?

Chapter 2

 I Was There When:

Stu Ungar won his final, and third World Series of Poker championship (Main Event). The Main Event is the gold medal of poker, with a $10,000 entry fee it is the dream of every professional and amateur poker player to be a part of this great spectacle. This was the first year that they played the final table out on Fremont Street, outside Binions Horseshoe casino, - and it was the last time. A canopy and misters spraying cool air was set up with bleachers for the watching audience. However, they did not account for the wind blowing in from across the desert down the enclosed street and the desert breeze wafted and twirled the cards through the air as the dealer dealt them. The dealer finished up sliding the cards across the table to the players, who had to physically hold down the two cards in front of them.

Stu Ungar won the event that year, and won $1 million - 9 months later he was found dead in the Oasis Motel downtown Las Vegas, with just $800 in his pocket. Ungar is thought by many to be the greatest poker and gin rummy player the world has ever seen. This quote by his friend and sometimes backer Mike Sexton from the book *'One of a Kind'* perhaps portrays Unger best:

'Stuey Ungar was the greatest gladiator in poker history. He took command of every table he played in and dominated his opponents heads up'.

He won and lost millions during his brief career, never having an address, a driving licence or a bank account to his name. The son of a New York bookmaker, he was at one time backed by the New York mafia, and was in fact although not a 'made man', but 'connected' through his friendship with Gus Fransca a capo (captain) in the Genovese crime family. Victor Romano, a foot soldier in the Genovese family became Stu's long time friend and over the years he treated Stu more like a son than a friend. In effect this made Unger practically untouchable in the murky arena of gambling whether it was legal or illegal either in New York, Los Angeles or Las Vegas.

I only saw him that once, but it was a privilege to see in the real person one of the greatest poker and gin rummy players that ever lived.

Johnny Moss is one of the legends of poker and was still playing poker and living in Binions when I first went to Las Vegas. Moss was one of the original Texas road players, who played the original form of Texas Holde'm during the 1930s and 1940s, playing in some of the biggest games around during this period. When his good friend Benny Binion moved to Las Vegas and bought the old Mint casino, Johnny followed him bringing the new format of poker to Vegas with him.

Moss was instrumental in Binion initiating the World Series of Poker. There is some doubt however, that the well famous incident of playing Nick the Greek Dandalos for the first World Series title in 1949 is in fact true. Moss did play Dandalos in a game set up by Binion, but it was at the Flamingo - Binion had lost his licence to run a casino, and did not get it back until mid April 1950. However, what is poker legend is the final words spoken by Nick the Greek, after Moss had financially ruined him at the table: *"Mr. Moss, I have to let you go."* In his book *'Ghosts at the Table'* Des Wilson investigated this incident at great length and came to the conclusion that it probably did not happen. Perhaps what is in less dispute is Nick Dandalos's other famous quote:

'The best thing in his life is gambling and winning; the second best is gambling and losing'.

I Was There When

What is also not in dispute is the fact that Johnny Moss was a great poker player of the old school. But along with that came an arrogance and a consummate desire to win at any cost, and this often put him at odds with other players and dealers. During his last days, Benny Binion's son Jack Binion allowd Moss to live in the Horshoe, and I was playing poker in Vegas during these days. I actually met Moss - well, not 'met' in the true sense of the word, rather he nearly ran me over in his wheelchair whilst leaving the poker room in Binions. Eyes, fixed straight ahead, driving at a far to greater speed that had any regard for safety, he was determined mow down any unfortunate pedestrian in his way. I could see the arrogance and self importance in his face, and although never spoke to him, could quite believe the stories told about him.

It was also at this visit that I met Anthony Holden and Al Alvarez. It was the day after Tony had signed his book *'Big Deal'* for me. We bumped into each other outside Binions the next day, and Tony introduced me to Al Alvarez. Of course, I only knew him from his excellent book *'The Biggest Game in Town'* and that he was a frequent player at Holden's Tuesday game. It was only later on when I started my Language and Literature Degree (I was a late starter in life!) that I realised who this little quiet man, with twinkling eyes indeed was. One of the great literature figures of our time, a friend of Sylvia Plath and her husband Ted Hughes the Poet Laureate. It was an honour to meet him and chat about poker. It was at this meeting that I made my usual gaff; Tony Holden had asked me about playing, and getting on with Americans in general on my visits to Vegas:

"Well, not too bad", I answered, "but after about a week they begin to annoy me, and I get a little sharp with them - they are ok in small doses".

It was not until later that day, that I realised, Tony's wife, referred to as *'The Moll'* in his book, was indeed an American. I met Tony some years later at the WSOP in the

I Was There When

Rio, and apologised for my crass remark made that day. He smiled and said it was ok, and that in fact he remembered the incident. I doubt if he did and was probably just being polite, but it made me feel good. It was an honour to meet them both.

In those days the WSOP was not just about winning the money, just as important was the honour of being named the World Champion. But it was also about entertainment, about having fun, excitement and putting on a spectacle. Every year Puggy Pearson who was one of the old Texas road gamblers would dress up in all manner of costume: Viking, Arabian Sheik and many other costumes. I was there the year he came walking into Binion's poker room dressed as a Native American Indian with full feathered head dress, smoking a large cigar. I saw his motor home which he would park outside Binions for the duration of the World Series, with the inscription on the side:

'I'll play any man from any land any game he can name for any amount I can count, (and in smaller print) - *provided I like it'.*

A start contrast to the modern WSOP were hundreds of grim faceless young men, most of them IT or Maths graduates sit round without speaking, staring at one another across the table taking an endless length of time to make a decision. They just do not have the panache or flamboyance of the old road gamblers, many like Benny Binion could not even read or write. These colourful characters bought the game to life and made it more entertaining than a Vegas show to watch for the less skilled amongst us. It was worth travelling the thousands of miles just to watch the final three days of the main event from the rails. Nowadays they play the final table up on a platform, with TV cameras festooned around, and bleaches twenty feet from the table making it impossible for the spectators to see. Somewhere along the passage of time, something personal has been lost from the poker community.

I Was There When

Despite the above it is still my must time to visit - during the six weeks or so over June and July when the World Series of Poker is taking place. It is the Mecca for poker players and although I do not play in the World Series anymore, Vegas is awash with poker players during this period which makes the tournaments and the games at other casinos bursting at the seams with poker players from all over the world. This has not gone unnoticed by the other casinos and many including the Venation, the Golden Nugget, Planet Hollywood and many more hold their own summer tournaments under a guise of different names on the back of the World Series during these months. As Johnny Kampis calls it in *'Vegas or Bust'*

'A summer camp for poker players'.

It also gives me the opportunity to see great poker players of the past and present playing at the highest level of the game for free. The atmosphere at the Rio at this time of year is second to none, and whilst walking down every passage way, sitting in every coffee shop you never know who you will bump into. Last time I was at the World Series I sat in the Starbucks coffee shop in the Rio and the great Dolly Doyle Brunson came speeding along in his motorised wheelchair and parked himself on the next table to me, nodded and said *"Good morning"* - a legend of the game.

I was also there when Huck Seed won the World Series in 1996 becoming the youngest player at that time to win the title and at 6' 7' one of the tallest. Seed is also known as the 'King of Prop Bets' for his proposition bets with other poker players, some of the most noticeable are:

- ❖ A wager of $50,000 with Phil Hellmuth that he could float in the ocean for 18 hours - he lasted 3. Others included:
- ❖ Running a mile in under 4.40 - he ran 4.47.

I Was There When

- ❖ Running a mile backwards in under 10 minutes. No information.
- ❖ That he could break 100 on a desert golf course five times in one day, by just using a five iron, a sand wedge and a putter - he won the bet on a day when the temperature was 120 degrees.

The year I watched Seed win the World Series taught me a lesson that was invaluable for me in the subsequent years. I still remember him sitting at the table with the $1 million in the cardboard box in front of him. It was tradition at the time for the $1 million to be placed in a card board box on the table between the last two players in the final.

Seed was dressed in T shirt, backwards turned baseball cap and trainers. It taught me to realise that at a poker table the players dress and appearance has absolutely no bearing on his/her ability to play poker.

Chapter 3

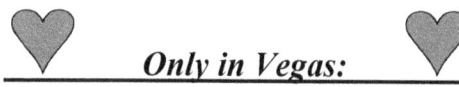
Only in Vegas:

I was in Las Vegas a few years ago when they suffered a fairly strong earthquake which measured 6.5. The epicentre of the quake was some 200 miles away in Eastern California on the border with Nevada, so although 6.5 is quite high on the Richter Scale there was not a lot of structural damage in Las Vegas. I had never been in an earthquake before and the novel experience bought the seriousness of this natural phenomenon home to me.

I was playing poker at the Excalibur casino when the seismic activity struck. There was no warning; no building up of the tremors, no noise; nothing. Without warning the heavy chandeliers over the card room started swinging from side to side; the poker table, which is a very heavy piece of furniture, starting jumping two three inches in the air and moving to the side, and all the slot machines, chairs etc started shaking. It takes a few seconds for the mind to register what is happening, and then my first reaction was to grip the chair arms and sit rigidly still.

The quake only lasted for about 10 seconds and I did not see anyone move from their chair. The strangest thing about this story is that the dealer Tim continued dealing the cards! Tim is a dealer who I know is a pretty much laid back guy who plays golf and travels to UK to play on the big golf courses in Scotland and England. But, this stretched his laissez-faire demeanour to the limit, as he continued to nonchalantly deal the cards across the now bouncing and moving table. Then to compound the farcical situation even more, the players (including myself) picked up the cards and continued the game. Only in Vegas!

Only in Vegas

The quake only lasted about 10 - 15 seconds and stopped just as quickly and without any warning as it had started. Immediately the shaking stopped and whilst continuing to deal the cards, Tim announced to no one in particular: *"Pass the sick bags"*. Now, Tim had obviously been in an earthquake before as he knew that one of the immediate side effects of these tremors is a feeling of nausea. I myself wondered at first what the hell he was talking about, until after a few seconds I began to feel queasy, a sensation that lasted for about 5 or 6 minutes. Others at the table commented on the same sensation, so I presume it is a common side effect of earthquake tremors.

A couple of days later I got into a conversation with an elderly couple from California and the conservation turned to the recent earthquake. They had been at home when it happened only arriving in Vegas the previous day. I learnt another piece of earthquake knowledge from them; they explained that they had not felt the tremors in their home town, despite being nearer to the epicentre than me. Coming from California they were obviously well versed in earthquake triva, and they explained to me that the after-effect tremors do not always travel in a circle from the epicentre as usually depicted on graphs. The tremors from a few days ago had travelled East along a straight fault line, and had not gone in any other direction.

I learnt many things from this experience, but one overriding thing was the hopelessness and fear that must engulf people caught in a serious earthquake. My experience only lasted 10 seconds, but during that short length of time I was frozen in my seat just trying to work out what was happening. When I have seen subsequent major earthquake events around the world at least, albeit in a small way, I appreciate the feelings and my heart goes out to them - there is nowhere to run.

I was in Las Vegas when every casino had a lounge bar, with entertainment that was in operation 24 hours per day. One of the strangest sights I saw in those early days concerned one such lounge bar. My first wife H and I had an early flight from McCarron airport to Atlanta, so we were checking out at around 4.30 am. Whilst walking through the Plaza to reception, we had to pass their small lounge bar, complete with stage and seating for about 30 or 40 people. There was a few die hards still playing the slots, and still a few around the craps table, but apart from these the casino floor was empty. On stage, with no one in the audience was a group banging out rock music with the lead singer talking and introducing the music to an empty space! If I recall correctly he was even making a few jokes to the 'empty chairs' - only in Vegas!

Another of the traditions that seem to have passed into oblivion is the 'happy hour' event, which most of the smaller casinos would operate at some time during the day. One of the most wacky took place at a small casino that no longer exists - O'Sheas Gambling Hall. O'Sheas, as its name suggests was a small Irish themed casino incorporated into the Flamingo directly opposite Caesars Palace, and was always packed with drinkers rather than gamblers, and I witnessed their 5pm - 6pm 'happy hour' first hand one scorching July evening.

Their 'happy hour' was in full swing and consisted of a real male dwarf, dressed as a leprechaun running along the top of the bar, pouring beer from a glass 'yard' into the open mouths of customers lined along the bar. The people were of course jostling and pushing to get to the front of the bar, which only contributed to the merriment and the high spirits of the occasion. With the leprechaun continually running backwards and forwards with foaming yards of free ale, the people cheering him on and everyone singing to the background music of Irish rebel songs it was the epitome of Vegas. The revellers could not sing along with *'The Fields of Athenry'* and if they could I doubt if they would have understood the social message behind the words, but hey who cares they were enjoying themselves - only in Vegas!

Only in Vegas

I had intended to finish playing poker for the day after leaving Caesars, but O'Sheas' small card room area was right at the side of this long bar and I could see that the players were in the same mood as the revellers at the bar, i.e., playing with gay abandon - I could not resist the temptation - I sat down to play. I played for about 3 hours and it was one of the most enjoyable nights poker I have ever had in Vegas.

Even the street vagrants are a different 'class' in Vegas. I do not wish to belittle the people in Vegas who live on the streets or make light of their situation, many of whom have just fallen on hard times in a hard city. Most of the vagrants who beg on the street have hand written signs in front of them with some humorous comments that you would not expect from those in such a sad plight, signs such as:

'Homeless; my wife has run off with my girlfriend - need help'.
'Why lie, I need beer'.
'I'm too ugly to sell myself - please donate'.
'Need a rich woman - enquire here'.
'Smiles are free'.

It of course conjures up the phrase: *'There but for fortune go you or I'.*

Another thing that seems to have become popular in recent years is the plethora of 'personal pleasure' apparatus in the shopping malls, casinos and nearly every area where there is space for them. I use the phrase above as I do not believe there is a collective noun for them. They include the massage chairs, with or without masseur, foot masseurs, high pressure water body cylinders, oxygen bars, and the latest I saw - vending machines with disposable soft shoes which apparently, according to the voice emitting from the machine, allows you 'to walk round the malls in comfort'.

The masseurs offer a range of massages on the specially adapted chairs ranging from a price of $40 - $100 depending on how much of your body you want pounding. They offer 'Swedish'; 'Japanese'; 'American'; 'Sporting'; 'Medical' types of massage - I have never understood the difference? I have on occasions availed myself of these services whilst walking round the casino or shopping mall - and I can assure the reader your upper body, arms neck and shoulders are bruised and pulverised in exactly the same way whichever 'style' you choose. I have sometimes enjoyed these 20 minutes sessions, but on many other occasions I have felt worse than I did before I sat down!

These masseurs also come round the poker rooms in Vegas and offer their services to the player at the tables. It is not uncommon to see a player with his chair turned round having a neck, shoulder and back massage whilst involved in the game. I have never had these massages whilst playing but it looks enjoyable and is on my to do list.

The best description of the above water jet apparatus I have seen is by Karlin when describing these at the WSOP as: *'A cylinder which appears to be a cross of an iron lung and a washing machine'.* Like Karlin, I have never seen the benefits of going through a wash cycle like a pair of dirty socks or underpants.

Similarly I have never seen the benefit of having two spikes stuck up my nose to suck in fumes from half a dozen tanks filled with coloured water of a dubious source. In many of these locations an attendant, usually female, young and attractive, will for an extra fee massage the breather's head with a claw like hair brush made of uncomfortable looking barbs. This is not on my to do list.

However, I must be honest and say that in the main, these 'pleasure apparatus' are well supported and invariably seem to be busy - perhaps the world is leaving me behind.

Another event that is popular in Las Vegas are the conventions. There are approximately 19,500 meetings and conventions held in Vegas every year. Many of these

Only in Vegas

are held and the Las Vegas Convention Centre which encompasses 3.2 million square feet under one roof, 13 exhibit halls, a lobby and concourse area with 144 meeting rooms seating up to 7,5000 and parking for 10,000 cars. These conventions are a double edged sword for small stakes visitors as myself; on the one hand they bring lots of people into Vegas, many who want to play poker but alternatively the price of the room hotel rooms can sometimes double, especially when there is a large convention in town.

One of my favourite times to visit is when the National Rodeo Championships are held in Vegas, usually first or second week in December, and with approximately 190,000 people attending in 2019, it brings a lot of cowboys and cowgirls into Vegas. It is a great event with a parade of cowboys and cowgirls on the strip and a massive trade show at the convention centre. To give the readers an understanding of the size of this convention centre, on one of the floors apart from around 1,000 stalls selling 'cowboy' goods (including guns!) there is a purpose built stadium holding roping, and bronco busting events.

I was in Vegas on 12th December 2015 when Connor McGregor fought Aldo for the UFC featherweight title. On that weekend, apart from the 100.000 + cowboys and cowgirls in town there was also an estimated 7,000 Irish men and woman who had come from Boston, New York and other parts of the USA, and Ireland to support McGregor. It was a fantastic weekend.

It is well known that the Irish can drink, but as I have witnessed also can the cowboys (and cowgirls). It is rumoured that the bars in the Mirage and the Nine Fine Irishman pub in New York, New York ran out of beer - but it was only rumour and I have no evidence - however, I was in both these casinos during that weekend and I would not be surprised. The great thing about this weekend was that I never saw any trouble through drink with the mixing of these two groups. Everyone was just enjoying the atmosphere.

I had met some of the Irishmen in Atlanta airport on the way to Vegas, and they had flown Dublin - Heathrow - Atlanta - Vegas and had paid up to $700 for their entry tickets to the fight. I myself had contemplated trying to buy a ticket to get into the fight at the MGM arena - I am glad I didn't - it lasted 13 seconds!, with a win for McGregor. I spoke to some of the Irishmen after the fight in the New York, New York - were they disappointed at paying out all that money and travelling all those miles for 13 seconds? - not at all, they just partied anyway, some of them did not even have a hotel room - they just slept where they sat. Only in Vegas!

One of the Vegas 'scams' I have witnessed over the years is the 'find the lady' game operated by very skilled card sharks. It is illegal to operate these games on the streets, so they usually set up shop on the pedestrian walkways over the Strip. They do this for various reasons (a) they have a lookout who is in a good observation position, (b) there is a lot of pedestrian traffic and (c) they are not patrolled by the casino security staff.

I think most of the readers will be familiar with the 'find the lady game' - but briefly; it is a fairground game in which the dealer has 3 cards; one of them being a Queen. The dealer then mixes up the cards and the punter has to try and find which one is the Queen, for any bet he wishes to put on. You cannot win - at best you will have a 3/1 chance of winning. These teams always operate in 3's: the dealer, the shrill and the lookout. The shrill is the person pretending to be a member of the public passing by playing the game and winning - this hopefully encourages innocent onlookers into the game who see someone winning.

One of these favourite places to set up these games is on the walkway between the Bellagio and Caesars Palace - I think this is because there are plenty of escape routes if they are seen by the authorities. During my earlier days as noted in the opening to the book, I was involved in the local Magic Circle and did a close up card magic routine, so I was well versed in these types of games and would watch with interest how good dealer was. In this particular game over this particular walkway the dealer was very good - but the shrill was hopeless! She was a tall black lady whooping and hollering every time she won a few dollars - her acting ability was one notch below zero!

"How can anyone be fooled by this?", I thought.

But they were - people where still betting on the cards, and of course the dealer let them win a few small stake bets. Then when they were tempted (as many were) to place a larger bet - they lost. Of course, I stood at the back observing without getting involved, and after a while I looked up knowing there would be a lookout somewhere. There he was standing at the end of the walkway - not walking or moving along with the crowd, built like a barn door and standing around 6'4". I could not resist - walking passed him I said: *"Hello, how you doing?".* He looked at me with suspicion, but with some trepidation did say:

"Fine".

"Look", I said *"I know you are the lookout, none of my business, but that shrill is terrible, you need to get rid of her".*

His faced dropped, and he was lost for words, but looked immediately over towards the game and the shrill who was still jumping up and down whooping and hollering. He mumbled something under his breath that I could not catch.

I smiled at him, said:

"Have a nice day", and walked into the Bellagio.

The above street scam should not detract from the many genuine, and in many cases good street entertainers that can be seen on the Strip and Downtown. They vary considerably from the costumed Micky and Mini Mouse, Darth Vador etc., to the excellent musicians and street

Only in Vegas

magicians. I would urge however, any new visitor to be careful of the costumed street vendors who invite the passerby to have their photograph taken with them. When these people first appeared on the Strip it was customary to give them $1 or $2 for a photograph - now they are demanding $20 - beware. Some of the musicians and magicians that perform mainly Downtown on the Fremont Street pedestrian area are very good and well worth a couple of dollars contribution.

Chapter 4

 The Dark Side of Vegas:

According to official statistics there are some 12,000 homeless persons in the Las Vegas Valley with many of them living below the city in the storm drains.

In his excellent book *'Beneath the Neon': Life and Death in the Tunnels of Las Vegas'* Matthew O'Brien gives an excellent portrayal of some of these homeless people who are the 'residents' of the rat infested tunnels that run beneath the streets of Las Vegas; their lives before the tunnels, their stories and their views on life. I can highly recommend O'Brien's book for any reader interested in this topic. In his book O'Brien notes that the above number of the homeless is suspect as it was taken on a one- night census and is considered to be low, very low, as it counted only visible people.

Las Vegas has 200 miles of flash flood tunnels running underneath the city with an estimated 1,000 people living in them, some permanently with beds, furnishings and shelves. The people are referred to in various terms, 'The Mole People'; 'The Drain Dwellers'; and they vary from full time employees in the city or the casinos who cannot afford housing, to gambling and drug addicts. This figure is also an estimate, and applies to the homeless who live permanently in the tunnels. It is logical to assume that both the above sets of figures are grossly underestimated.

A billion or so years ago the Las Vegas Valley was an inland sea surrounded by mountains, so the rain that falls naturally runs into the valley below. Despite being in the middle of the desert, Las Vegas suffers infrequent but often heavy instances of rain thereby suffering regular flash floods.

The Dark Side of Vegas

During the Spring, air from the Gulf of Mexico produces thunderstorms that release large amount of rain and the solid valley floor allows very little infiltration. The rain can fall some 15 miles away in the mountains, so by the time it reaches the lower regions of the basin it is a raging torrent moving at 30 mph filling the above tunnels and washing away everything and everyone in its path. Anyone inside one of the tunnels is trapped with no way out until the next exit or entrance point further along the tunnel which may be some 2 or 3 miles away. Similar to O'Brien I could find no official estimate or record of the people drowned or washed away in the tunnels through the flash floods. However, considering the statements made by many of the dwellers that when it rains heavy the people in the tunnels only have a few minutes to vacate, the number who do not make it must be considerable.

The tunnels are even segregated by the occupants into separate areas for drug addicts with areas for heroin, crack or meth; and another section of tunnels for gambling addicts. There is no lighting in the tunnels, and the only light comes from the flashlights the residents have - if they can afford the batteries. They have no way of knowing whether it is night or day, until the light shows at the end of the tunnel. It is ironic in that this is probably the only thing the dwellers have in common with the gamblers in the casinos above them. O'Brien remarks in his book also on the similarity between the storm drains and the casinos above them when he says:

'Walking into a storm drain is like walking into a casino: You never know what's going to happen, but the chances are it isn't going to be good'.

The tunnels run under some of the largest, top of the range casinos on the strip, zig zagging across the Boulevard and the Freeway; and I have played poker in most of these casinos. I find it mordant that when the revellers are drinking and gambling in the neon of the Vegas casinos (I include myself in this), they do not realise that just 200 feet below them destitute and desperate people are living in squalid conditions in constant fear of their lives. People who are living alongside the rats, the snakes, venomous spiders and with the ever present threat of death by drowning.

In an investigation by Alison Maloney for the Sun newspaper in August 2019 one of the employed dwellers, John Aitcheson, who works shifts in a convenience store on the Strip said:

'I could get an apartment, but all my money would go to rent, food, electricity, water. By the time I was done there'd be no money left over to do anything'.

Another employed inhabitant of the tunnels mentioned in O'Brien's book is Harold. Harold has lived in the tunnels for around two years and is an ex truck driver who lost his licence. He is working 4 or 5 days a week for a fencing company, working as and when he wants to. He cooks himself two or three meals a day on a stove in the tunnels, sleeps and goes out to work at night. Harold had just got his licence back and he is saving money and hopes to have enough to get an apartment in 6 or 7 months time. He does not drink, take drugs or gamble; for him living in the tunnels is purely economical.

Most of the inhabitants stay in the tunnels during the heat of the Vegas day and trawl the casinos at night looking for credits or coins left in the machines by the daytime gamblers or searching the skips outside the casinos for food - termed 'dumpster diving' by the dwellers. Some of the more determined of the gamblers amongst them will only sleep in the tunnels at night and spend the day gambling in the casino sports books, where they can gamble for small stakes, but get free drinks.

Some of the residents come and live in the drains for other reasons than drug or gambling addiction. In an article of September 2019 for the Insider Magazine 54 year old Rusty said:

The Dark Side of Vegas

'I used to have an apartment and lived on welfare, but because of my husband's past no landlord would accept us anymore. We have been married for 12 years and I didn't want to leave him, so I went into the tunnels with him'.

Rusty and her husband, plus two dogs have lived in the tunnels for 5 years.

One of the strangest stories courtesy of O'Brien is that of Gwen and Tyrone. Tyrone was not a work shy man, he had slept in a car for a while and walked 12 miles every day to work in the Aladdin casino and eventually found a place to live. After taking accumulated leave from the casino he returned to find he had been laid off. He took to the tunnels to live.

Gwen was his mother, but Gwen did not live in the tunnels; in fact she lives in North California part of the year and the other part in Atlanta. She had lost touch with Tyrone and had been searching for him for 28 years, through private detectives, tracing agencies and search programmes, finally finding him through a database after his arrest for a small criminal offence. Gwen visits him from time to time hauling a suitcase full of gifts for him: new boots, flashlights, a suitcases and plastic bags for his clothes, backpacks and a new umbrella for the sun or the rain. The time that O'Brien met her she had flown in from North California and walked in 112 degree heat across the desert terrain, down into the wash and into the tunnel.

The amazing end to this story of O'Brien's is that after Gwen found her son, who she obviously loved, she offered him a home with her in Atlanta - he refused. Tyrone was an intelligent man with no mental health problems, he does not drink except a little at the weekend and only smokes a small amount of marijuana. So his reason for not leaving Las Vegas?; that although he appreciated her support, he felt that he had to work things out for himself and did not want to lean on her for support. God had put him here and God would help him get out of it and he was happy at the moment with his lot in life. Happiness is not material, but a state of mind.

After writing his book on the tunnel dwellers O'Brien started the non-profit organisation 'Shine a Light' that provides water, food, clothes, blankets, drug counselling and other services for the people sleeping and living in the tunnels.

It would be discourteous to the authorities in Las Vegas not to mention that they take this problem seriously and are trying to accommodate these unfortunate people and look after them in the best possible way. The motive for this may of course be questionable; is it merely to 'clean up the streets', so they do not visually offend the tourists, or is a genuine social feeling for fellow human beings? Whatever the motivation the Clark County officials have introduced a law stating that all new residents in Las Vegas must have: (a) a driving licence, and (b) not be in receipt of welfare - this in a hope to curtail the number of homeless.

Another positive move has been made by the casinos. Have you ever wondered what happens to the tons of food that is left over at the end of each day from the massive casino buffets? Large amounts of the food that cannot be stored or used again is sold off to various animal farms in Nevada, but some is also distributed to the homeless in Las Vegas. It is obvious that neither of the above will solve the problem of homelessness and street begging in Las Vegas - but it is step in the right direction.

During my many discussions over the poker table with local Vegas residents some of whom become friends over the years I cannot recall any mention of this darker side to Vegas. Whilst of course the locals know of the existence of drugs, prostitution and homelessness in the city they do not see it as part of their lives. I do not think this is a deliberate ruse to 'brush it under the carpet', I think it is more that this side of Vegas is a different life and part of the 'sin city' image that they do not belong to.

The Dark Side of Vegas

During my times in Las Vegas I have spoken to many of the people begging on the streets of Las Vegas, whether or not any of them lived and slept in the tunnels, I do not know; but suspect that many did.

Only once have I donated to anyone in Vegas begging on the street, and I think that was more out of guilt than any other sense of moral sentiment.

I had been playing in an afternoon tournament in the Sahara and came fairly high up in the final payout. I can't remember the exact amount, but seem to remember it was around $700. I went into a Wendy's burger restaurant across the street and had a much too large a meal washed down with a ice cold Budweiser. Leaving Wendys Diner I saw a young woman with four young children, the oldest being around eight years of age, and the youngest around eighteen months in a push chair. She was stopping people asking for money for food for the children, saying:

"That they had nothing to eat all day".

Of all begging sights I have seen in Vegas that was one of the saddest I have seen. She, and the children were poorly dressed wearing just shorts, flip flops and T shirts, ill kept and obviously undernourished.

I walked past, as most other people on the sidewalk were doing trying not to look her in the eye. However, I just could not get the sight of the children from my mind, and as I approached the next junction I stopped, turned round and went after her. I stopped her and gave her some money for food for the children. I made her promise me that it would go to feed the children and not on beer or drugs. I can still here her words ringing in my ears after all these years in a Southern American drawl:

"Thank you sir, thank you sir, thank you".

I asked her how she was in this position, and she told me that she had come from South Georgia with her husband a few months ago, but he had left her and the children, and she had absolutely no idea where he was, what to do or how to earn a living.

The Dark Side of Vegas

Maybe I was naive, and maybe that is how she made a living, but I like to think not and that day those children had a decent meal. I also, question my actions as I don't usually give to street beggars in Vegas; would I have done the same if I had not won that money in that poker game the same afternoon? I doubt it; it was the guilt of having that extra money without working for it, and giving someone in need the benefit of it.

I arrived in Vegas some two months after the public sale of cannabis was legalised on the 1st July 2017. I had expected to see drug induced gamblers and tourists 'zoned' out in the casinos and along the strip - but no there seemed to be very little difference on the streets or on the gaming floors. Anyone visiting Vegas who wanders of the general tourist areas cannot fail to see the drug addicts, both young and old. Over the years I have seen many lying comatose in alley ways, side streets and at times on the walk over bridges that span the strip and at times it has been very tempting to give assistance and to see if these poor souls are actually still alive.

I will at this point mention what happened to me recently whilst crossing the strip on a scorching hot Vegas day. The Strip (main road through Vegas) is very wide - in fact in places it is six or seven lanes - each way!, and although the lights have seconds indicators informing the pedestrians how many seconds they have left to cross, you still have to move pretty quickly to get across in time. On this particular occasion I was somewhat negligent and had to run the last few yards across the road - tripped on the curb and fell quite heavily on to the pavement. I lay there quite shook up and with a painful shoulder, ankle and hip. I expected one of the hundreds of people walking the pavement to stop and at least ask if I was ok. No one stopped, in fact I distinctly remember two groups of people stepping over me whilst I lay prone on my back!

I could not believe this, but realised afterwards they must have thought I was a drunk heavily under the them here - one a voluntary organisation and one a public one.

One of the many voluntary and Christian organisations that are helping to solve this problem is the Salvation Army, who run programmes giving the victim a new skill and start in life. Known as the 'Salvation Army's Seeds of Hope' programme it offers a 24 hour hot line plus clothing, shoes, and transportation to a safe place. Their web site notes that:

'The programme works in collaboration with the local law enforcement agencies, the FBI, ICE and other community service providers to identify, rescue and restore victims of all forms of human trafficking'.

The programme also helps victims who may also have substance abuse problems.

Mike Shoro reporting in the Las Vegas Review-Journal in February 2019 noted a new team of law enforcement agencies and groups that has been formed to combat sex traffickers and to assist the victims of trafficking - The South Nevada Sex Trafficking Multidisciplinary Team. The team gives the Clark County School District and other victim groups a say and an input into what happens, with medical, mental health services, education, transportation and emotional support all coming together for their needs.

The other 'darker side of Vegas' is of course the sex industry and prostitution which is given some sort of degree of official approval by Vegas authorities. The fact that you seldom see women soliciting on the streets, or seeking clients from a car, does not mean that it never happens and as you will read later, often happens in the casino bars or gaming floors. Gladly to say I have no experience of this during my many visits to Vegas, other than what is noted in Chapter 3. It may surprise many people to know that in fact prostitution and brothels are illegal in Las Vegas and Clark County. People who wish to avail themselves of this 'service' (and I know many who have) then they have to travel over the county line to such establishments as 'The Cherry Patch', 'Mable's Whorehouse' and 'The Chicken Ranch'. Many of these establishments have become so famous over the years that they sell souvenirs; T shirts; posters; coffee mugs and car bumper stickers - only in Vegas! - well, just outside Vegas.

I do not mind the homeless or the drug addicts on the streets of Vegas - they don't bother me and I don't bother them - although some of these unfortunate people are not a welcome site for the visitor, they pose no threat. One of the things however, that does annoy me on the streets of Vegas are the army of men and women thrusting sexual advertising leaflets into your hand as you walk by or whilst standing in a queue for the bus. A number of years ago the Vegas authorities cracked down on these people, many were arrested and the harassment stopped. However, in recent years it has gradually crept back in and although not as bad as a few years ago it is making a comeback. These leaflets contain phone numbers with dozens of adverts for girls:

'Not a dull moment with me'; 'Sexy older woman'; 'Exotic dancers and stripper' - all 'direct to your room'.

What annoys me is this is prostitution under another guise which the authorities tolerate, and yet on the other hand they are desperately trying to advertise Vegas as not only a gambling destination but also a family one.

I do have personal knowledge - not experience - of how some of the girls noted above operate. I friend of mine who used to play in the above mentioned house game in Blackpool was victim to one of these scams. He was returning to his room at Treasure Island late one night when two young black girls got into the lift at the same time. They asked him if he wanted to come back to their room for some 'fun'. My friend (who was single) naively agreed. Once he had shown willingness for this venture, they switched and said that it would be better if they went to his room, as they had another friend in their room that might not be too happy with it. Again, naively he agreed.

Once in the room one of the girls pulled a small bottle of whiskey out of her bag and poured them all a drink -

"Just to get in the mood", they said.

The next thing my friend remembers is waking up some 3 or 4 hours later - the girls had gone - and so had his wallet.

As noted above it is very rare to see a prostitute on the streets in Vegas they do not proposition their clients in view of the authorities or the police. Neither in my 30 years of visiting Vegas have I seen them 'cruising the street' and propositioning people from their cars - as is often depicted in films. Working girls usually work the casinos and to avoid recognition only staying in any casino for ten or fifteen minutes before moving on, and never proposition or approach a prospective client more than a couple of times in any given casino. The casino employees; dealers, pit bosses, cocktail waitresses etc, obviously get to know any local girl over time but turn a blind eye to events and take the view that the girls *'are only trying to make a living'*.

You may be wondering at this stage - 'how do I know all this?' Part III - *Charlene the Hooker*.

Vegas is inundated with strip clubs, topless bars etc; and many of these are advertised on the sides of buses, taxis and boardwalks. In 30 years I have only been in one of these establishments once. And that was at the request of my second wife J. One of these strip and topless bars was situated on Fremont Street and J and I would pass it on numerous occasions when we stayed at the Plaza hotel at the top end of Fremont. One night she asked if:

"We could go in and take a look".

Some of these establishments charge an entrance fee at the door; some charge a fee but you get it back on the first drink; some do not charge but insist you buy at least 2 drinks during your stay and have security to make sure this happens. This particular bar was the latter of these with no door charge, so we went in. There were strippers on the stage in various stages of undress and topless waitresses

The Dark Side of Vegas

walking round delivering drinks. J thought this all amusing and wanted to wander round taking it all in as just another Vegas experience. However, she was not so amused when I ordered two bottles of beer - actually both for me, as J did not drink. The two Budweiser's came to $25 > $12.50 each + tax, which is four times the usual price for a bottle of beer in a Vegas casino bar.

I politely declined the two beers and departed the bar without any further glances at the scantily clad women on view. It was an amusing experience that J and I laughed about for years after, but I (we) never went into a strip or topless bar again.

Sex is advertised and offered in many areas in Las Vegas. I love to go for a massage whilst in Vegas, and on one occasion I visited a well advertised, and what I thought, a reputable establishment. It was very nice: reasonably priced, clean with showers to take before and after the massage, security for your money and possessions and pleasant Asian staff. The massage was good, music and subdued lighting and lasted an hour. At the end of the session the young Asian girl turned to me before I rose from the table and said:

"Do you want me to send you home happy?".

Of course my gambler's mentality kicked in straight away, and I am thinking *"Reduced rate?"; free vouchers for next visit?"; "two for the price of one?"*.

"Only another $75", she said, noticing my quizzical look.

Then the penny dropped. *"No thank you"*, I replied, getting quickly off the table, *"The massage was good, that's all I wanted"*.

She smiled and said: *"OK - you come back again soon"*.

With that I gave her a tip and left.

Chapter 5

Vegas Casinos:

You could be forgiven for thinking that the cost of a hotel room in the entertainment capitol of the world would be expensive. On the contrary hotel rooms in Vegas tend to be inexpensive because many of the hotels make their primary income from the in house entertainment; gambling, restaurants, shows and shopping areas. Most of the casinos in Vegas do not need to charge high room rates to make a profit. One of the few remaining 'perks' for the regular visitor to a particular casino is the upgrade on the room. Most casinos have differing level of room comfort and luxury, and all them have records of visitors who have stayed there over the past 5 years. I think this is a US legal requirement. Over the years I have invariably been upgraded in casinos that I have visited on more than one occasion. But, to be honest at my low level of gambling the upgrade is not of any significance, and on many occasions I have not noticed any difference in the room, other than it is in a different room section of the casino - a different tower.

However, the obsession to make increasingly yearly profits by the big corporations who now own the casinos has led to a couple of unpopular charges to tourists and locals alike.

The first one which was introduced around five years ago is the 'resort fee'. This is a percentage fee on top of the room rate and typically works out between $35 to $45 per night depending on the room. The casinos claim that is for other amenities in the hotel, such as: the swimming pool, wi fi connection, use of the gym and a free daily newspaper. It is of course a legal rip-off, as you still pay even if you do not use the gym, or the wi fi and the most absurd of all you still pay when the swimming pool is closed in the winter! There is no escape, unless you earn points through the casinos rewards loyalty card - I do not pay the resort fee if I play 5 hours a day of poker in the casinos card room. I do not make those hours over the week, however, the hours are totalled and I get a percentage reduction, usually around ten to twelve days on a two week trip.

The second charge to be introduced recently is that of paying for parking at the casino - even if you are staying there! This also affects the locals who have given their custom to the casino over the years and now find themselves paying for parking. Again, there is a way around it by playing a lot of hours and building up your rewards loyalty card to the next level, which allows free parking and amongst other things free buffet tickets.

The problem is that different casinos operate different rules in regard to the above charges even if they belong to the same corporation. An example for the small stakes poker player is that the Mirage and the Excalibur both belong to the MGM corporation, but have different rules regarding the resort fee. If I play at the Excalibur I can get it reduced, but at the Mirage I cannot, but can get a room reduction rate by playing the same 5 hours of poker per day, but only if the hotel is paid in separation to your flight. So to anyone from abroad who has a package deal, it does not apply.

It is difficult to say why the casinos in Vegas differ so much in the amount of gambling and action that takes place on the gaming floors. I have stayed at the Excalibur for my last six or seven visits to Vegas; whatever time of day it is a lively, loud casino floor with most of the table games and roulette wheels in full action most of the day and night. The shopping arcade is busy with the restaurants and cafes doing a good trade. The poker room usually has four or five tables in operation, with at least one continuing through the night.

However, if I walk across he Boulevard to the Tropicana it is almost empty with very little action and gamblers virtually non-existent. Both casinos are in the same location, and are roughly in the same room rate price range.

The Bellagio is situated on the centre strip and is one of the top of the range casinos in Las Vegas (this is where they made the film Oceans 11). The action is similar to the Excalibur, although I suspect with a majority of high end gamblers (I once saw Morgan Freeman gambling here) always busy with a tremendous atmosphere and a poker room that has waiting lists a mile long.

However, if I walk across the street to the Venetian, the gambling and gaming is much less in evidence. Although the Venetian is always busy, most people seem to be taking in the ambiance of the place and the extensive but expensive shops. It does not have the same 'gambling' atmosphere as the Bellagio across the road.

It is difficult to assess what makes a first-rate casino; each has its own peculiarities and things it can offer to the visitor.

The two busiest casinos in Vegas downtown, the Golden Nugget and Binion's Horseshoe are across Fremont Street from each other and they are at the opposite ends of the casino spectrum. The Golden Nugget is modern, bright, glitzy festooned with silver mirrors and a spectacular swimming pool and caters for the high end of downtown visitors. Over the now pedestrian Fremont Street the Horseshoe is a dark, low ceiling, no frills gambling emporia, with no limit betting but only a small roof top swimming pool.

Both casinos are always full of serious gamblers enjoying the cheaper rooms, bars and cafes of the Downtown area.

It must be noted however, that the Horseshoe has declined somewhat over the last few years since the Binions family shut down the hotel part of the casino and sold it to Caesars Entertainment Corporation. It is alleged that Caesars only wanted the World Series of Poker rights, which they then moved to the Rio casino. From that point on very little enterprise was put into the casino and the hotel itself. It would be remiss not to mention that in the early days the Binions success as a casino was built on Benny Binion's philosophy of concerning itself with the needs and wishes of the gamblers. No frills, no shows, no cabarets, no fancy decor - just gambling - the only sop he gave (as mentioned elsewhere) was free drinks to the gamblers. The revenue in those early days of Binions outstripped that of Caesars Palace. This attitude can best be summed up by a quote from David Spanier's book '*All Right OK You Win*' by Binion's wife Teddy Jane:

'*Who cares about the decor at the Horshoe? it looks like wall to wall people to me*'.

The Horseshoe was the only casino in those days (and possibly still is) that would take any bet. It is a well documented story of William Bergstrom who walked into the Horseshoe in September 1980 with 2 suitcases, one containing $777,000 in cash (777 being considered lucky by gamblers) and the other empty. With Binion's permission he place the whole amount on a craps table, won the bet, stacked his winnings into the empty suitcase and disappeared. Then in November 1984 he returned with a suitcase contain $550,000 in cash, $140,000 in gold Krugerrands and $310,000 in cashier's cheques. Again he bet it all on the Don't Pass Line on the same craps table - but this time luck was against him, and Bergstrom lost the bet.

The last time I played poker in the Horseshoe was some three years ago. I used to like to play in the Sunday afternoon tournament which in years gone by would always attract 70 or 80 players. The poker room had been

Vegas Casinos

moved some years ago to the old sports book area, and although not the same as before it was still satisfactory. On this occasion, the poker tables had gone and a sign at the entrance said it had moved to a location near the Keno lounge. On arriving at this destination my heart fell; just three tables. I looked in bewilderment, at the member of Binion' staff who I supposed was the 'card room' manager.

"Is this it?", I inquired.

"Sorry, sir I'm afraid it is", he said in a similarly disappointed tone of voice.

He was as clearly disappointed as I was at the demise of this great poker icon. Anyway, I stopped to play this Sunday afternoon tournament with a $70 buy in. There were nine players - my heart was not in it - I got knocked out early, left and never returned. On my subsequent visits to Vegas I have stopped going into Binions Horsoe - it saddens me to witness both the demise of the casino itself and the loss of the once famous poker room and coffee shop - both of which have gone. I like to remember it as it was in those early years.

The casinos in Las Vegas have obviously changed over the years that I have been visiting. They have changed along with a changing society and clientele, changing to meet the needs of the visitors and changing along with the economic and financial situations of the time.

When the Circus Circus casino and hotel was opened in October 1968 it was one of the first casino properties to court families, and it still remains their modus operandi today. The building itself was designed as a massive big-top tent, and everywhere you will find clowns, children's magicians and entertainers, with a full circus show operating twice daily. There is also a large Adventuredome - a huge sprawling indoor amusement park with a go-kart track and a multitude of other attractions for adults and children alike.

Over the years as Vegas moved towards a more family oriented destination other casinos also incorporated children's themes into their hotels and some of these are mentioned below:

Mandalay Bay has a huge 11 acre water park with beaches covered with tons of imported sand. There is a wave pool and an endless Lazy River on which you and the kids can float on inner tubes for hours.

The Excalibur has the Tournament of King with jousting matches featuring knights and kings There is a Fun Dungeon which is a sort of combination of a video arcade for youngsters, and a carnival.

The Mirage has The Secret Garden, the Dolphin Habitat, and until recently the White Tigers of Siegfried and Roy, and of course it has the volcano that explodes every night. The Mirage also has pools that contain waterfalls, lagoons, rafts and private cabanas for families.

Most of the casinos now have gymnasiums or fitness suits to cater for the younger generation of tourists and of course the aforementioned pool parties. I do not have a problem with this - if anyone of any age wished to avail themselves of this, then it is ok by me. However, what annoys me is that I am paying for this through the compulsory resort fee - it would seem much fairer to me to charge on entry for this extra service. I am already paying for the swimming pool and internet connection that I very rarely use - OK rant over!

One of the thing that has not changed however, is the size of the casinos.

It has always been hard to explain the sheer size of some of the casinos to friends and family who inquire and some of answers to these can be seen in the 'Vegas Trivia' parts of this book. However, to add things of a more personal note I would give a few details of some of my experiences of the size of some of the casinos I have visited or played poker in.

The Shopping Forum at Caesar's Palace is huge. You can access Caesars by many different entrance points, one of them is through the Shopping Forum. My first wife H and myself accessed this point on our first visit for a 'quick look round the shops' before we went into the casino - it took us nearly 5 hours! - we entered at 1.00 and eventually got into the casino around 5.00. The casino floor is as equally large.

I love Caesars Palace, I have played a lot of poker there both in the old card room and in the new card room which is situated next to the massive sports book. Everything about Caesars is luxurious and I love just walking around the place and taking in the opulence. I find it one of the most difficult casinos to get around - a couple of years ago I found a nice quiet coffee shop in Caesars that sold pastries etc. On my last two visits to Vegas I have tried in vain to find this coffee shop again; walking round and rounds in circles until finally giving up and going to Starbucks. As mentioned elsewhere, there are 18 restaurants and eating places in Caesars.

In the middle of the gaming floor is the circular high limit room. Unlike many high limit rooms in Vegas the general hoi polloi are allowed to walk through this room, and I do regularly, and as I walk through I think that this is where Frank Sinatra got into a brawl with Caesars casino manager who eventually pulled a gun out and threatened to shoot Sinatra. Sinatra was playing the Palace and was given $10,000 free each day just to be seen playing on the gaming floor, and the fight started when Sinatra caused a ruckus because he wanted more credit.

The casino manager was eventually arrested in his own casino by his own security guards - only in Vegas! I walk passed this area and think of a different world.

No Vegas casino has windows (except at the front entrance), no clocks, no exit signs and no straight and navigatable routes through the casino floor. On our first visit to Mandalay Bay H and I spent an hour just trying to get out. Even now when I visit Mandalay Bay I struggle to find my way out, and usually finish up by asking an employee for directions. Another feature of the Las Vegas hotel rooms is there is no coffee or tea making facilities - they want you down on the gaming floor gambling - not sitting drinking tea or coffee in the room! None of the windows in Las Vegas rooms open - the suicide rate in Las Vegas is about three times that of the national rate - they don't mind if you commit suicide, but do it elsewhere please, we don't want the bad publicity. The Venetian, along with the Mirage is one of the Vegas casinos that use scented air conditioning to relax and sooth the gamblers on the casino floor.

One day, just for curiosity I decided to walk the length of the MGM grand. I walked at a steady amble from the Strip entrance, through the casino floor, through the food court and the shops to the swimming pool at the back of the casino. It took me 20 minutes - I figure that is not too short of a mile. The walk through routes are not, as mentioned above, straight in any Vegas casino, so the distance maybe a little shorter in a direct line. However, I stopped at the swimming pool, if I had continued into the MGM convention centre rooms you could add at least another 10 minutes on to that time.

Even now, after all these years at the Excalibur I frequently have to stop and get my bearings when walking through the casino, and often find myself in the wrong place. I use the location of the various gambling sections, bars or cafes to navigate my way around all the casinos I frequent. The Sports Book, the Cashiers Cage, the Central Bars or Starbucks are all my signposts to steer my way around the winding unending paths through the casino.

No clocks or windows also makes it difficult to know the time when in Vegas. Vegas is a town where day blends into night and night back into day without the punter knowing, or actually caring. The vast majority of gamblers in Vegas go to sleep when they feel like it - irrespective of the time of day or night - clocks are superfluous in Las Vegas, all you need is a body clock.

Vegas Casinos

Located in a prominent position on the Strip, Circus Circus is a massive casino incorporating a full circus ring with a couple of dozen 'bunko booth' style games - darts, camel racing, ring throws and the above mentioned Adventuredome. All this size does not include the shopping and restaurant areas also under the casino roof; all this is hard to comprehend in trying to envisage the size of an average Las Vegas casino.

In the past Circus Circus had very vibrant Poker Room with a variety of cash games and tournaments, plus plenty of free food always on the go. For many years it was my usual Saturday afternoon place. The circus ring and bunko booths always made a relaxing break from the poker during these sessions.

One of the largest poker rooms I have played in is situated in the Venetian, another casino of gigantic proportions and along with its sister casino the Palazzo is one of the most luxurious casinos in Vegas. The twin complex is the second largest hotel in the world with 7,000 rooms and suits costing between $169 to $10,000 per night.

The Venetian has a canal complete with gondoliers which runs through the casino, taking about 20 minutes to complete the ride with the gondoliers singing throughout the journey to the 'passengers'. Although I have never been subjected to this ride, I have witnessed it hundreds of times, and it seems to me that on the majority of the times the occupants of the gondolas are embarrassed at the gawking observers such as myself gazing down from the ramparts during the journey.

It also has a full size replica of St Mark's Square in Venice with an Italian mini opera show twice a day. It is one of my musts to take in this show at least once on my visit to Vegas, sitting with a coffee from a nearby Italian cafe listening to these authentic Italian opera singers is a splendid and relaxing way to spend an hour.

Vegas Casinos

Much is made regarding the 'eye in the sky' - the cameras in the Las Vegas casinos -

'Every where you are, someone is watching you' (Julia Roberts ~ *Oceans 11).*

If people do not think this is true, think again, and I can give two good examples of this.

The Excalibur moved the card room a couple of years ago, and I was one of the players in the first game to be played in the new location. We all moved from the old room and sat at the table, but it was hours before they allowed the game to start, why? - they had to reposition the cameras because the control room could not clearly see every hand that was played by every player at the table.

The second example comes from my early days in Vegas. I do not play slot machines, but H and I realised that if we did, we could get free drinks. Now, I am not so cheap as not to buy a beer (I think), but we tried this complimentary just for a laugh, a bit of fun to see if it worked. What we did was look at the path the cocktail waitress was taking with her trolley, sit at machine in that path and pretend to be putting quarters into the slot machine whilst rattling a few quarters in a cup.

Sure enough it worked, and we did this a couple of times getting free beers (apart from the tip) in the process. However, after about 30 minutes two big burly security guards appeared from nowhere like genies from the preverbal lamp and stood behind us. Now, in those early days all the casino security guards were in uniform and carried guns, so to put it bluntly - we got out of there very quickly and never tried it again!

One thing that has improved in the casinos over the years is the quality of the poker rooms and the games available. There is less selection than during the poker boom years, but it has become a question of quality over quantity. Every poker player in Vegas will have his or her favourite room, or at least a couple of equally favourite rooms. I have played in all the current high end rooms except the Wynn - not for any particular reason, I have just not got around to it. I would urge any new poker player who visits Vegas for the first time to play at least once in one the top poker rooms - Aria, Venetian, Bellagio, Caesars etc - they will find he experience invaluable in their poker progression. For the first time low stakes poker player it can be very intimidating to play in these card room, but if you play carefully, tight and follow your plan I think you will be pleasantly surprised - I was.

There is less selection of games than ten or twenty years ago; but there are still plenty of games available to the first time visitor who wants to play low stakes poker - both cash games and tournaments. The Flamingo run a $2 - $4 limit game; The Mirage and the Excalibur run $3 - $6 limit and spread games, and all the casinos run $1 - $2 no limit games. These games usually run 24 hours a day. Low entry tournaments can be accessed from a variety of casino card rooms from $40 - $100, with the number of daily tournaments varying from 4 a day to just one a day.

I try to divide my weeks in Vegas between playing serious and 'just for fun' - the $2 - $4 games in the Flamingo noted about are strictly 'fun' games, with plenty of tourists drinking and simply enjoying themselves. You are never going to make any serious money by playing in these games. So, if I am feeling a little 'poker lagged' I will spend an evening in this card room just to enjoy the conversation, banter with the Americans and not worry too much about skill, strategy etc.

The Mirage $3 - $6 game is also an enjoyable game, and after the Circus Circus poker room closed I made this my regular Saturday afternoon game. It is a well run game with friendly but professional dealers and a good mixture of regular players and tourists. I remember on one occasion on my last visit sitting down at this game, and at the table was a well dressed elderly lady who was regaling the table of her life experiences. She was not at the table long and so I missed most of the stories, but she was

Vegas Casinos

married to one of Frank Sinatra's backing group of musicians and had been telling of the 'old days in Vegas' when the Rat Pack were ever present and their exploits.

If I want to move away from this fairly relaxed atmosphere then I can always move up to the $1 - $2, $2 - $, or $2 - $5 no limit games. These games are sometimes just as relaxing, but the play is much more serious with players paying more attention to the strategy and finer points of the game. The casinos where I currently play most of my cash games are: the Mirage, Excalibur and the Flamingo with occasional sorties to the Bellagio or MGM.

I very rarely play the low entry tournament games that are offered in these casinos. It is an arena where new players want to try it out - often encouraged by the card room manager. There is nothing wrong with this, and it is an excellent idea for the first time visitor to Vegas to get involved in poker. Usually these entry fees are around $40 so no one is going to lose a vast amount of money. To learn the game and get the experience of playing in a Vegas tournament is well worth the money.

The casinos where I can find a higher entry type of tournament are: the Aria, Caesars Palace and the Mirage and apart from infrequent visits to other tournaments in the Venetian, MGM or Harrahs this is where I currently play most tournament games.

If I am in a tournament it is with the sole intention of winning - not just to pass time and have some fun. I want to play with serious players of around the same skill level as myself and I restrict myself in Vegas tournaments to entry fees in the $100 - $200 level. I have found over the years that these attract players of the same level of play as myself, and of the same attitude towards the game as myself. They are usually tourists with a few residents who are pleasant and communicative, but know the game, the etiquette, the rules and take their poker seriously. One of the other differences between casinos that the first time player in Vegas should be aware of is the blind levels and the entry fee and starting chips.

It may seem generous to get a large amount of starting chips in one casino compared with another for the entry fee. However, if the blinds (small and large) are increasing faster so consequently this starting stack is going down quicker.

For example: The MGM grand may give you 10,000 in starting chips for $60 but the anti's and blinds are going up every 10 minutes. Whereas the Mirage may only give you 5,000 starting chips for $60 but the anti's and blinds are only increasing every 20 mins, so which is the best deal? I would like to note that the above is only an example and not the actual case for the casinos mentioned. These starting chips and blind levels vary tremendously between casino to casino and the beginner needs to decide on which suits them best. Personally, I prefer the system where you get a small amount of chips with a longer increase of the blind levels. Rightly or wrongly I believe this gives me the opportunity to play tighter in the early stages of the tournament, which is my style of tournament play - live or online.

I believe this variety of games is essential for the survival of poker in Las Vegas, both for the tourists, the small stakes professional grinder and for the local poker players.

Other financial incentives that is offered by different casinos vary to some that are permanent to others that run for a set period of time. These vary greatly depending on the ingenuity or creativity of the card room manager. I will just note two below as examples:

Excalibur:

The Excalibur card room has a large wheel with a variety of sections ranging from $100 to $25, table splash, double up, or spin again. So, if a player gets Aces 'cracked' i.e, his starting hand of AA is beaten in the hand then the beaten player gets to spin the wheel, providing there is at least $12 in the pot. This provides a dilemma for the player with the AA- does he try and win the pot, or does he try to lose and take his chance with the wheel. Of course, the player cannot disclose his hand to the other players, so many subterfuges had sprung up in the Excalibur card room to get around this problem, e.g. the player holding AA will deliberately and with obvious intent continually ask the dealer:

"How much is there in the pot"? - so making it obvious to the other players 'in the know' that he has AA and so let's increase the pot.

If the player with AA loses then he/she can spin the wheel and whatever amount the wheel finishes on - that player gets. If the wheel lands on 'table splash', then $100 is added to the next pot in the next hand on that table. If the wheel lands on 'double' then the player spins the wheel again and the amount is doubled.

When I was last in the Excalibur they had a promotion on that ran for 3 months. The deal was; if a player got a running flush twice in any 24 hour period then they would receive $200 from the casino. This was obviously a financial ploy to pull players into the card room, but it was good and added a little excitement to the game.

Mirage:

The Mirage have a similar promotion to the above Aces 'cracked' - but it only runs up to 1pm - this is obviously to attract players early to the game and to get the tables up and running for the day. This is a permanent promotion. One of the varieties of this is that the player can forego the $100 for a chance of win a larger amount of money on their rolling jackpot, which is a virtual 'slot machine' located in the card room.

Vegas Casinos

The Mirage also had a promotion that ran for a limited amount of time in which a table number would be picked out at random by the card room manager, then the manager would pick, again at random, a seat number on that table - the player in that seat would win $100 dollars. It was a very popular occurrence and would be greeted by a round of cheers for the player who won the money. However, it only applied to the cash game tables and not the tournaments.

Vegas Casinos

Vegas Trivia

Ceasars Palace, a classy but not particularly large casino, has 18 restaurants, and the pool area covers 45.5 acres.

The mini bars in Vegas hotel rooms have sensors that track the length of time the items are removed, and charge you after an elapsed time.

It is illegal to sell lottery tickets in Las Vegas

There are over 15,000 miles of neon tubing in the city.

The Nevada State Prison in Carson City had a casino for the inmates for 35 years from 1932 to 1967. It was finally shut down by a new governor from California.

Over the years some strange things have been banned in Las Vegas, they include: Hula Hooping; Megaphones; walking a pet on the strip, hip hop concerts and giving food to homeless people on the street.

The Dunes hotel was the first casino in Las Vegas to have a topless show. However the Nevada State Legislature was not in agreement and made a new law stating that the women could not move while topless.

Chapter 6

Getting Married in Vegas:

Las Vegas averages around 150 - 300 marriages a day; no waiting, no documents - which is very attractive to drunken gamblers and celebrities alike.

There are hundreds of different ways to get married in Vegas, some of them verging on the bizarre. They range from a drive through wedding on a Harley Davidson, to speaking your vows whilst on the New York, New York roller coaster. From sky diving 'chutted' together, or bunging jumping with the minister to underwater marriages at the Silverton salt water aquarium.

You can also get married at Denny's Diner for $199; which will include the wedding official, use of the diner's chapel, a pancake wedding cake, a champagne toast and two breakfasts - only in Vegas.

I had originally not meant to include this chapter of my life in these ramblings, however, on reflection I realised that these same procedures are the same for everyone. I thought it would be good for the reader to understand the simplicity of marriage in Vegas.

J and I were married, in a rather ordinary way compared to some of those above and perhaps, mundanely at the Little White Wedding Chapel on the strip. The only claim to fame in this, is that Frank Sinatra and Mia Farrow; Bruce Willis and Demi Moor; Rita Hayworth and Dick Hames; Paul Newman & Joann Woodward and a long list of other celebrities were married there too. The official photographs of their marriages deck the walls of the Wedding Chapel; I don't think mine would have made it. I must go back to find out one day!

Getting Married in Vegas

I had booked the marriage ceremony online before leaving for Vegas; and the grand cost of $200 included: pick-up with white stretch limo from the hotel; 12 official photographs (album $20 extra); make up and bouquet for J; button hole flowers for all the party, and of course last of all the ceremony itself. I thought this was a good deal!

Before you can get married in Vegas you have to get the licence from County Hall at a cost of $55, so the day before we went to do this. We arrived at the County Court and stared - surely this can't be the right building? The steps were littered with hung-over drunks and it seemed all the flotsam and jetsam of Las Vegas. After we weaved our way through this minefield of human rubble who were waiting on the County Hall steps to attend the criminal court in the same building, we entered a small reception area. A sign directed us to another vestibule where on a table was a cardboard box full of stubby little pencils, a pile of forms, and an instruction to 'fill in the form, and take to counter'.

This we did and followed another sign to the line up for the counter. The line up was quite odd to say the least - behind us was an American couple with a small child in a pushchair; they were dressed in shorts, flip flops and Hawaiian type shirts. It gave you the impression that they had been out shopping, and just thought: *"Hey; let's go and get married."* Behind them was a Japanese couple - he was dressed in full morning outfit complete with bow tie, and she was dressed in a full length white wedding dress - a true Vegas mixture!

We arrived at the counter and pushed the pencil completed form under the glass partition to a very pleasant looking lady who checked it, made sure it was signed, pressed a few buttons smiled and said:

"Your licence will come through that hatch in a couple of minutes; have a nice day".

Now, J had a few years earlier changed her name by deed poll, I had been divorced, so we had both brought

Getting Married in Vegas

along with our passports and proof of UK residency, a whole other batch of official looking documents to prove who and what we were.

"Is that it"?, I said looking somewhat bemused "is that all"?

"Yep, that's it - your'al done", she said smiling through the glass.

She had obviously seen this all before; the simplicity of getting a marriage licence in Las Vegas; it was easier than renewing your car road tax at your local Post Office! We wandered back through the human rubble on the steps not quite at ease at how easy it had all been.

The following day we got married the at the Little White Wedding Chapel on the Las Vegas strip. The stretch limo picked us up from the hotel on time for the short journey to the North end of the strip. In the reception area we saw the same Japanese couple, still dressed in the same outfits as the day before. Neither of them could speak a word of English - the receptionist was trying to tell them that they had to pay extra for the album that contained their wedding photographs. I don't think you got a translator for your $200!

The first thing was the official photographs, which were taken in a studio inside and then some others taken outside in the Chapel's grounds. The actual ceremony itself was a little comical, and nearly as bizarre as the previous day's events at County Hall. We were first asked if we wanted a civil or religious ceremony, we decided on the religious.

"Ok", said the receptionist, *"through that door over there is a wedding chapel, go stand against the door and wait"*.

We waited - Steve 'The Womble' Walmsley (previously mentioned from the Early Years) arrived with his partner, and went and sat down at the front of the chapel.

In due course, one of the biggest black guys I have ever seen, came through carrying a transistor radio. I think the civil versus the religious was just in the type of clothing the marrying official wore. This guy was dressed as a traditional pastor complete with dog collar and apart from that I could not determine any difference.

"J.....and Mike", he asked.

"Yes"

He went to the front of the chapel, said hello to Steve and switched on the transistor radio. Out came a rather scratched version of 'Here Comes the Bride', and the pastor waved us down the aisle. When we arrived in front of him he switched off the 'music' and shouted in a deep, booming Southern States voice:

"Lordy, Lordy, we are gathered today to witness the ...."etc;

J looked at me, I looked at J, and it we had great difficulty in not breaking out into fits of giggles.

In due course we were officially married, went out to the reception area to receive the official photographs that had been taken before the ceremony, and signed some sort of official document. Steve witnessed the signatures and that was that. We walked around the Stratosphere for a while, and then went to the Sahara coffee shop for a burger, fries and a coke. I often wonder if Elvis (married at the Aladdin), Frank Sinatra or Bruce Willis had to fill in their forms with stubby little pencils, and then stand in line to get their marriage licence; I like to think they did.

Part III: Characters and Friends

Shanghai Lil
Charlene the Hooker
The Perfect Retirement
High Rollers
Non Gamblers
Vegas Trivia
Friends

Chapter 1

 *Characters:*

Shangai Lil

One of my strangest experiences in Vegas happened at the old Sahara Casino. I had wandered into one of my favourite coffee shops in Vegas and the receptionist had asked me to wait just five minutes whilst a table was being cleared. As I sat down in the reception area I notice a Chinese lady also waiting, sitting alone. Attractive, perhaps mid-forties well-dressed sitting demurely in the corner smiling. Subsequently the receptionist called me through, and Shanghai Lil (for want of a name) stood up, tags along and followed me to the table. *"Strange"* I thought; but said nothing, and neither did she. The receptionist was walking away from us so she did not see this.

Of course the waitress who then came to the table obviously thought we were together and asked to take our order.

"I will have the burger plus fries", I said, *"but I don't know what she is having"* pointing to Lil.

Lil smiled and said to the waitress:

"Just juice" in very broken English, but said nothing to me - just the smile. When the waitress had left I asked her:

"Are you waiting for someone?".

Again in broken English: *"It is ok - I wait for you"*.

So now I am really thrown. She continued to smile through it all, with me trying to work out the situation. *"Was she a hooker?"* I asked myself, *"Does she have a mental health problem?", "Is she trying to get a free meal?",* but none of these seemed to fit the situation.

"Oh, right", I said, *"But what is your name - do you live in Vegas?".*

"My name Lillian I come from China".

"Oh -ok - are you with some one?"

Still the smile and: *It is ok - I wait for you"*

At this point I am thinking it is some sort of scam, and had visions of a huge beefy Chinaman rushing through the door making a beeline for my table with a large meat cleaver.

Nothing more was said and after a few minutes the waitress came back with my burger and a juice for the lady.

Then when I was halfway through the burger, she stood up, smiled and went through a door at the back of the coffee shop. I thought that is the last I will see of Lil. However, 10 minutes later, when I had finished the burger and was drinking my coffee, she came back carrying a plastic carrier bag (which she did not have before), sat down at the table finished off the juice and smiled. Now I am even more perplexed. Lil sat quietly for a couple of minutes then stood up and said in broken English:

"*I go now",* and walked out the coffee shop.

I sat there totally bewildered trying to work out what had just happened. Some 20 years later, I still haven't worked it out! My only thoughts are that she picked some free food up from a contact in the kitchen and she needed a reason to be in the restaurant part of the coffee shop, and it was me! I cannot believe she did all that for a free orange juice.

Characters

Charlene the Hooker:

It was the only time (I think) in my 30 years of travel to Vegas that I was accosted by a lady of the night. There I was minding my own business in New York, New York, contemplating whether or not to enter the rather noisy central bar for a beer. *"By me a drink",* came this sweet voice from behind.

Turning around I saw the most unlikely looking hooker you could imagine. A plain, but pretty looking mixed-race girl, the real 'girl next door' deal. No makeup, and wearing touristy looking clothes; shorts and top, aged around 30. My first thought was: *"God, she must be having a bad day to pick on me!"* My second thought was – *"undercover cop!"*

"No", I said *"They would not let me in there, I am far too young".*

A blank expression of dismay clouded her face, she must have been thinking *"Great, I have picked on a right nut case here".* I smiled, she smiled, realising it had been a joke.

"Well", she said, *"I have a room here if you want to come up".*

"Absolutely no", I answered. *"Only $100"* she said.

"Absolutely no", I reiterated. *"Anyway, I have a daughter much older than you". "No way am I coming to your room".*

"Age doesn't matter", she said, smiling very demurely.

We talked for a while and after about five minutes parted with a smile and a wave. What a really pleasant young woman, I thought. Whatever made her fall into that way of life.

At one corner of the gaming floor in New Your, New York is an escalator that leads to the walkovers to the MGM Grand one way, and the Excalibur the other. At the plaza at the top of the escalator is a small bar that overlooks the gaming floor. I headed that way, ordered a beer and sat down to do some serious people watching. After about five minutes, Charlene the Hooker came walking past the bar, saw me, waved and started to come in the bar. Immediately, the barman ran to the bar entrance, put his hands up to her somewhat like a policeman on traffic duty, and shouted *"No – out!"*. Charlene looked over at me, and the barman followed her glance.

"It's ok", I said *"She is with me"* (still to this day, don't know why I did it). The barman relented, and she came in and sat down at my table.

I bought her a beer and we sat and chatted for about ten minutes as if we were old friends catching up on the news. She told me her name was Charlene and she lives in Los Angeles.

"What, you come up here every day to do your hookering?", I asked.

"No, I work in an office in LA", she replied with a very fetching smile, *"I take time off work for about four days every month and come to Vegas to earn some serious money".*

"I think we are two of a kind Charlene", I said.

"How's that?"

"Well, I'm an amateur poker player, and not a good one at that, and seeing on how you had to proposition me, you're an amateur hooker and not a good one at that!"

Charlene laughed. We were getting on well, and it was one of those situations in life where you think that in a different time, and a different place things may have been different. Or maybe it was the Vegas atmosphere that was messing with my thoughts.

At the very least, she was persistent and asked me again if I was sure I did not want to come to her room,

"Only $100", she smiled.

"Nope", I said, *"not interested".*

After a while and more chatting, she smiled and said:

"Ok Mike, I have to go and try and earn the cost of my trip, nice to have met you".

I gave her a hug, and told her to be careful out there. She waved and walked out the bar.

Later on that evening in the Excalibur I saw Charlene again, this time from a distance. She was in her 'working clothes'. Expensive looking evening dress, high heels and makeup which advertised her profession. I was standing at a roulette table watching some very drunk young Americans being relieved of their money at a remarkably swift rate, when she passed by. She smiled, waved and gave me the 'thumbs up', voicing "good luck" from a distance and went on her way.

I am still not sure, after all these years if indeed she was an undercover vice cop. There are a lot of them operating in Vegas, in an attempt to clean up the city. A couple of things puzzle me: Number one: if the barman recognised her straight away, she is obviously a regular; so, how was she allowed to book a room in New York, New York and go through the reception procedure which is very tight in Vegas. You always have to register a debit/credit card in case of any unpaid hotel costs, or the resort fee. Number two: the cost she quoted was very cheap for a Vegas hooker. It will cost you $70+ at a cheap massage parlour for a Swedish massage, so $100 for whatever she was offering did not seem quite right to me. When walking through the New York, New York casino I often think of Charlene the Hooker, and wonder where life has taken her. I hope she is ok.

There was another occasion when I think I was propositioned by two young black girls in the MGM Grand. Because of the jet lag I am always awake very early the day after arrival in Vegas. This particular day I was up early and walked for a while in the cool of the early morning, and whilst walking through a very quiet MGM at 5.30 in the morning I passed two girls dressed in evening wear.

Characters

"Do you want to have some fun, hon?", one of them said.

It was 5.30 in the morning! Were they early starting hookers?, or trying to salvage something from the dregs of a bad night? I looked at my watch, did not say anything and walked on - I think they got the message.

The Perfect Retirement:

Whilst playing poker at Harrah's one afternoon, I heard a commotion from another table. Looking over I saw a loud obnoxious player a little worse for drink was causing problems for the dealer. However, he wasn't the one I noticed, as sitting next to him was a small quiet man smiling through all the furore. He was very brown and with wrinkled skin from a life in the sun with a mop of black hair framing his thin face. He was casually but smartly dressed with an air of serenity surrounding him. The fracas ultimately died down and all returned to normal.

The next day I was walking in front of the Bellegio lake and fountains. It was hot - very hot with the sun at its highest. Sitting on the pavement, under a tree seeking respite from the searing heat was the very same quiet man sitting with a little can, begging. Well, not actually begging, I don't think his pride would let him do that. He was selling for a dollar each, little drawings he had done on scraps of paper. My curiosity got the better of me. I knelt down beside him and bought one of his little drawings and respectfully said:

"Look, yesterday you were playing poker in Harrahs, now you are sitting here peddling these drawings, what gives?".

He looked at me with a smile on his face and said:

"Well, it's like this, every month I get my welfare cheque; buy enough food for a month, pay all my bills for the month, and what is left I play poker with every day".
"Then if it runs out before the next cheque, I come down here and do this until the next cheque comes".

I met him a few days later in Harrah's card room. He was waiting for a seat at the cash table and I was waiting for a tournament to start. He introduced himself as Jake and after a bit of 'poker talk' I asked him if he came from

Vegas. He said that he came from Los Angeles and he had come to Vegas around 5 years ago - he could not remember exactly. He confided in me that:

"He had had a little trouble with the law".

He never actually said, but I suspect that he had been in prison. He told me that during his life he had been a big drinker and had skated very much close to the line on what is legal and what is not legal. From my experiences as a Prison Officer, I would guess that he had been a petty criminal all his life and possibly subsequently been in and out of prison most of his life. There was no evidence for this - it was just a gut feeling fostered by my own experiences.

One thing that did surprise me is that he said that he never drank now, and over the couple of weeks I saw him in Harrah's poker room, I never saw him drinking at the table - although it would have been free. He had been married a long, long time ago and he had children somewhere, but he had no contact with them, and indeed did not know where they are. Unfortunately, this is a familiar story of many inhabitants who have moved to Vegas to forget or leave a depressing life behind. He was an engaging man and like many I had seen in the prisons of the UK pleasant and congenial with a resigned air about him, and acknowledgement that this is where life has led me - so I am making the best of it. He seemed happy with the life I have described above, and my feeling was that despite the loneliness it was better than the one he had left behind. I still have his little drawing; it is pinned on my message board in my study. I hope he is ok.

Another perfect retirement conception came from a similar looking character I met whilst playing poker in the Plaza, Downtown. We got to acknowledge each other after playing for a few days in the same games. After a few days the nods became talk and after the usual poker chat, such as: where you from, do you live in Vegas? – this alerts you

Characters

to locals who are grinding it out everyday hustling the tourists – he told me his story.

Him and his son travel around, spending a couple of months in each city or town staying in motels. His son, who I later met when he came to pick his dad up, is a joiner who can easily get work on building sites in any area they decide to stop whilst he plays poker most days. In the evening they team up and play poker together. Most of the cities they stay in are in the Southern United States, because as he explained - there is always building work going on even throughout the winter and they don't have to worry too much about clothes etc.

He never mentioned a wife, or ex wife, but he did mention that they do have a permanent home in Pittsburgh and sometimes when the travelling and motels get to them, they would go back and spend a few weeks in the property. Neither did he ever mention his past employment or job, but from the texture of his skin - sun soaked and leathery - I would guess that he had worked most of his life outdoors. He was a very curious man, and wanted to know all about England, how we lived, what we ate etc - personal, not political issues and I found him a pleasure to talk with. But in keeping with his life style he was there one evening playing poker - next day gone - and despite many visits over those early years, I never saw him again. Like the earlier retiree he seemed happy with his lot.

Chapter 2

High Rollers:

I was waiting for a poker tournament to start in the Monte Carlo one Sunday afternoon, so to pass the time I sat down for a beer at the bar just outside the poker room. Sitting at the bar was a man, perhaps in his fifties, well dressed and playing one of the virtual poker games that was embedded into the bar structure. All bars in Las Vegas have some sort of gambling machine set into the bar with most of them being simple 25c slots. He was cursing at the machine, and muttering to himself about his luck.

"Not having much luck", I said, opening up the conversation.

"Dam machines", he said *"Never seem to have much luck with them"*.

We chatted for a while, and I told him I was waiting for the poker game starting at 2pm. We went into conversation about the WSOP that was in progress at the Rio at the time.

"You a poker player?", I asked.

"Yep, but not good enough to play in the WSOP; but I am going down later today, I am backing one of my friends who is playing and I am putting up 50% of his $10,000 entry for the main event".

He explained to me (in a non bragging or condescending way) that he was the owner of a large farm machinery business in Oregon and had worked hard during his life and achieved near millionaire status. He enjoyed his poker but preferred to back better players in the big games. After some more cursing at the 25c machine, he finished his beer, said goodbye and went on his way. I sat there for a while trying to understand; I had seen this very rich, cordial and sociable man cursing because he had lost a few 25c bets on a machine. He probably had rolls of $100 bills in his wallet. Gamblers mentality!

This highlights another custom that has crept into the realm of the high stakes poker players over the years. That of 'putting themselves up for sale' i.e, giving a sponsor a percentage of their winnings, either over the course of a year, or for a single tournament for a percentage of their buy-in. They will also have a small stake in other players, rather like a bookmaker laying of his bets. It is very rarely that a player will have invested all of his own money in a high stakes tournament with $100,000 + buy-in. Exceptionally rich people with a good knowledge of the game and the high stakes players, will invariably have 'a piece of the action'. The variance in tournament play is so high that it would be almost impossible for a high stakes player to continually play tournaments that require high dollar buy-in.

In an interview for the Las Vegas Sun, professional poker player Darryll Fish said:

'There were times I won large scores and collected little to none of it - it is hard when family and friends congratulate you on winning, but you know you didn't get any of it'..

It is not often that lowly small to medium stake poker players such as myself get to witness a truly high roller up close, other than high stakes poker players. It happened as I was walking through the MGM one evening. There was a mild disturbance, with raised voices coming from a regular blackjack table on the main casino floor. I could see a couple of people standing round looking at the action, so wandered over to see what was amiss.

Seated alone at the table was a man, perhaps around 40, dressed in black T shirt, track suit bottoms and trainers. Not unkempt, or shabby, but certainly not dressed in the style of the high rollers in the other part of the casino usually reserved for them. In front of him on the blackjack table was $90,000, still in the $10,000 bound bundles, as if they had just come straight from the bank.

The argument was between the man, the dealer, and eventually the pit boss. The pit boss wanted him to put the money into his personal account with the casino - the usual procedure for players with large amounts of cash - but he was having none of this. He stood his ground, and eventually got his way, and we all watched in amazement as the dealer had to count out $90,000, and push it all into the usual money slot on the table and push across to him $90,000 worth of casino chips. These table money slots are narrow, so the bundles of $10,000 had to be split and stuffed down the slot at roughly $1,000/$2,000 at a time. Both the dealer and the pit boss were fuming. The T shirted player sat patiently with a look of satisfaction on his face.

He was betting $1,000 or $2,000 a hand, and after watching for about 30 minutes I wandered away and I remember that by then he had lost about $30,000. He was not playing to the audience or acting conceited; he never acknowledged the dealer or the people gathered watching - he just got on with his gambling. Whatever his background, and wherever he got his money from, he was just a gambler following his desire to win, whether he needed the money or not.

Maria Ho is a Chinese American professional poker player turned presenter who is amongst the best female poker players on the circuit and has mixed it with the best players in the world. Now, I apologise for any offence given here, but Maria is a very attractive woman, and when they were giving out female assets she was definitely at the front of the queue. Furthermore, she is quite happy to put these assets on display at the poker table which gives rather the wrong impression of Maria's personality.

High Rollers

In his book *"Vegas or Bust"*, Johnny Kampis cites the time he was playing in the WSOP and was seated at the same table as Maria Ho. He goes on to explain here such:

'Watching her work was a marvel. Despite possessing a kind smile and a sweet Cali (Californian) accent, Ho is a menace on the felt, every bet considered. I found Ho's stare among the most piercing I have seen'.

I was watching a high roller tournament at the Bellagio in which Maria was playing. There was a break in the game, and Maria left the card room for a while. When play recommenced she had not returned to the table and was nowhere to be seen. After a couple of minutes she came running from the casino floor eager to get back to the game, but was stopped by an old couple who asked if they could take a photograph of themselves with her. Instead of brushing them aside, she stopped, had her photograph taken, signed a book for them and chatted to them for a while before carrying on to the poker room and the game.

Now, to the poker disadvantaged this may not seem very much. But any poker player will tell you that during that absence from the table Maria could have forfeited not only her blinds (see Appendix), but also may have missed a couple of goods hands that could affect her position in the game. I witnessed all this from close range and it seemed to me to be another, albeit smaller, example of a poker player's good and charitable nature.

Whilst watching this same game I witnessed a good example of the high stakes poker players temperament and a natural quality that appears to always needs to be in competition. It is also an indication of how these professional poker players are held in esteem by the casinos in Las Vegas. A well known young American poker player by the name of Dan Smith had just been knocked out of the tournament. I have watched Dan Smith many, many times in high buy in tournaments and to me he seems one of the most quite, pleasant players on the circuit.

High Rollers

The game had been going for 2 days, so you would expect that someone who had just been knocked out to go and rest, relax by the swimming pool, or some such activity. But no, Smith set up a small folding table just outside the card room and commenced to play a serious game of chess with another player. There was no money on the table, but I would take it for granted in was for a substantial amount of money. I knew it was serious, as they had a timer to restrict the thinking time on the table and there was no friendly banter between the two. Not only that, after about 15 minutes two waiters appeared pushing a trolley loaded with silver dishes and platter (the real 'silver service') and proceeded to serve the two players lunch.

Chapter 3

Non gamblers:

Not all people come to Vegas to gamble. I was sitting talking to a lady in Starbucks in the Mirage, who with her cases in front of her was obviously checking out. She was waiting for her husband to come down from the room and we chatted for a while about gambling, Vegas etc; but when I asked her what games her husband played she laughed.

"No", she said *"it is me who plays the slots; we have been coming to Vegas twice a year for 30 years, and in that time he has never gambled a penny on anything - not a dime!"*.

When I was taking my A levels (I did this later than what is the normal in life), the English Language teacher was also a lay Methodist preacher, and quite high up in the Diocese. I bumped into him and his wife one day in Preston and after chatting for a while, I mentioned that he looked very suntanned, and asked him if he had been 'somewhere nice'.

"Yes", he answered with a knowing smile, *"Las Vegas for a couple of weeks"*.

He went on to explain that his wife and himself went every year to Vegas, just for the sun, to relax, go on tours and see the shows. Not every Vegas visitor is a degenerate gambler!

Two of the most non gambling types I met in Vegas was a couple from Somerset who had only come because their daughter was airline cabin crew and had got them virtually free tickets. 'Fish out of water' goes nowhere near enough to describe this typically English couple. I never got their names, but they told me they came from a rural village and had never been to America before. The lady was sitting on a long seat inside the 'Miracle Mile Shops' - a large horseshoe shaped shopping mall. She was around late fifties, with the pale, delicate skin of an English country lady; dressed in a flowery dress, with no sleeves, cut off the shoulders and wearing no hat, and fanning herself with a handkerchief.

It was midday in July, and the mercury was hitting around 108f in the shade on the strip. She was obviously distressed, and when I inquired if she was ok, she explained to me that her husband was in a nearby shop trying to buy an umbrella of some sort to protect her from the sun. I tried to explain to her in a respectful, gentle way that this was not the Costa del Sol, and she really should not be walking around like that under the Mojave desert sun without any cover. No wonder she was feeling faint!

Eventually her husband came out with a large floppy hat, and after some initial chat, he said that he at least wanted to gamble a little on his first, and probably last trip to Las Vegas. The conversation went something like this:

"I would like to play that pontoon game, we used to play it when I was a lad".

"You mean blackjack - you realise there is a method of playing that, with something known as basic strategy".

"Well, I don't know what it is, but we used to call it 21, and you could either stick or twist".

Now I have a problem, I can be kind and tell him, yes it would be nice for him to go home and tell his friends back in Somerset that he had gambled in Vegas, or I can be cruel, tell him the truth and save him embarrassment. I decided on the latter. I told him that if he sat down and did not play basic blackjack strategy, the other players at the table would be a tad more than 'miffed', especially if his ignorance of the basic rules of the game caused the dealer to win and them to lose. In addition, if he said "stick" or "twist" instead of the recognised hand signals, he would be considered to have some sort of affliction that is unknown to American gamblers, and be treated accordingly.

"Oh", he said, with a bewildered look on his face, *"Perhaps I had not better play".*

"No", I said "Stick to the slot machines".

His wife then said that she was feeling faint, and wished to go back to the hotel room to lie down. I bade them farewell, and left.

Vegas Triva:

The first casino in Las Vegas received its gambling license in 1931.

43 percent of Nevada's general fund is fed by gaming revenue.

William Lee Bergstrom placed the biggest (known) bet in Las Vegas when he walked into Binion's Horseshoe with $1 million in a suitcase and placed a $1 million bet on the roulette wheel - he lost!

The biggest pay out (so far) on a slot machine was $39.7 million won at the Excalibur in 2003 by a 25year old software engineer from Los Angeles.

There are 22,000 conventions held in Las Vegas each year.

Cannabis for recreational use became legal in Las Vegas in 2017.

There are 2,200 gaming and slot machines in Caesars Palace.

Chapter 4

Friends:

It would be remiss of me not to mention some of the other friends I have made on my trips to Las Vegas over the years. They include people I have met and talked from year to year, and although not having a story to tell, they are important to me in my memories. People who on seeing me would say:

"Hiya Mike, nice to see you - how long you here for"?, or, Hiya Mike, when did you get in"?; Hi Mike, how's things over the pond?

Perhaps it is presumptuous of me to call them friends, but I like to think they are.

Over the years I have built up a good British versus the Yanks relationship with many of the poker players I meet on a regular basis in Vegas. It is only because I can call them friends that this table banter, and as the Yanks call it 'joshing' or 'bullshitting' can continue in fun and kept to the correct perspective. Over the years I have often been asked by American poker friends and other players at the table:

"Why to do you come to Vegas so often Mike to play your poker?".

My stock answer to this has been:

"To get some desert sun on my back and to listen to you people mangle my language".

I have found over the years that this never gets a negative response, and it is taken in the spirit in which it was meant. In fact, on the majority of occasions it leads into a friendly discussion about the differences in language and the well known Bernard Shaw quote:

'The United States and Great Britain are two countries separated by a common language'.

Another of my stock answers to this question - but only to those who know me well, is:

"Well, I am here on behalf of the UK government to see how you have made out after Independence and if you people wish to return to the British Commonwealth".

This again, usually leads on to a friendly discussion about The Boston Tea Party etc, and generates a lot of good natured banter at the table. In all my trips to Vegas I try to keep in mind that I am a guest in their country, and everything is communicated in this vein.

One rather amusing evening that happened because of this professional friendship between myself and the Excalibur poker room staff occurred when a particularly loud and near drunken English player arrived at the table. On hearing my accent he said in a loud cockney accent:

"Oi, where you from mate?".

As is my usual, I ignored him.

"Oi, where you from mate, you a Brit?".

He was sitting in the next seat to the dealer Mary, who winked at me, leant across and whispered in his ear:

"He can't tell you he is on the Witness Protection Scheme".

Now, it is obvious to all that anyone on the WPS is not known to anyone - but this player was either to drunk or to stupid (I think it was a bit of both) to realise this, and Mary and I kept this going all night. I was a Mafia informant on the run as a contract had been put on my head by 'the boys' from New York - he fell for it hook, line and sinker - a great night!

Others at the Excalibur who I am happy to call friends are Eric the card room manager; and Karen, Tim and Edwin dealers from the Excalibur. Rae Ann is the dealer noted above from the Excalibur who over the years has picked me up from the casino on Sunday mornings and

Friends

taken me to her church, dropping me back at the casino at the end of the service.

Players like little Bill, ex poker dealer from Texas who worked on the oil rigs in South America and plays poker every day from 5pm until 8pm, when he goes to the gym late at night when it is cool. Except Thursday when he goes to his wine appreciation society to test the latest wines. On first sight, Bill will always greet me with:

"Here comes the Brits again, to take us poor American's money".

Greg, the ex reporter and sports book analyst who had his own show on American Radio and is a friend and neighbour of Mike Tyson.

One of the characters who I played against at the Excalibur for a few years was Janet, a local girl. Janet obviously had mental health problems but was tolerated by the card room manager, dealers, local players and others like myself who got used to her antics over the years. If she lost a pot, or had to fold her hand she would smack herself quite hard across the face. If she made a bad play and lost a pot, she would smack herself and then get up in a rage and stalk around the card room and run out to the ladies room (what she did in there I don't know). If this happened on two or three hands on the run, she would snatch up her chips, run to the cash desk and slap them down on the counter, take her money and run out of the card room.

Janet was also a heavy smoker and in the early days it was acceptable to smoke in the card room and at the table, fortunately this is not the case now. She would chain smoke cigarette after cigarette and blow smoke into her neighbour players faces quite oblivious to this obnoxious behaviour.

The last time I saw Janet was a few years ago when she rushed out of the card room after losing a pot, but collapsed on the casino floor. I think she had a seizer or a fit, but the paramedics were called and she was taken away in an ambulance. She obviously loved playing poker, but her smoking and behaviour caused mixed feelings ranging from amusement through to annoyance at the card table. I hope she is ok.

Non poker acquaintances like David who has an ice cream parlour in New York, New York. David is of Irish descent, and I pass his ice cream parlour most days walking through New York, New York to the strip. We chat mostly about boxing and UFC, and generally put the world to rights.

Johnny, a very dapper well dressed local who can be seen at one of my favourite bar/coffee shop 'people watching places' in the Paris casino. To escape from the heat of the day I would sometimes walk through the Paris and Ballys to get through to the Flamingo. On one such I day met Johnny who stood at the bar drinking coffee, and I got into conversation with him when I stopped to watch Wimbledon on the bar's large TV screen. Over the years I have stopped and talked to him many times about living in Vegas, the city and the people, politics and life in general. He is a engineer from the mid West who went through a traumatic divorce and decided to *'cut and run'* (his words) and change the direction of his life completely. He had never gambled in his life, he sold everything he had left after his divorce and retired to Vegas for the weather and the cheap living - still does not gamble, but runs early every morning before it gets too hot before going home, showering and getting dressed up for his day around Vegas.

At first glance you would take Johnny to be in the entertainment business, every time I saw him in the Paris he was dressed immaculately in a powder blue jacket and cream trousers. This attire was topped off with a cravat tucked into a pristine white shirt and finished with a pair of black and white spats. With his tall slim frame and brushed back thick white hair he looked the very imitation of a Cary Grant or David Niven. He was obviously a man of

Friends

routine as no matter what day I wandered into the Paris he was there - standing at the centre bar drinking his coffee. He then spent the rest of the day walking and talking in other casinos, and although I did not ask, he obviously had a particular route and locals he conversed with throughout the day. I am not quite sure if this constitutes a perfect retirement, but Johnny always seemed happy with his lot and I cannot remember him ever complaining about his current situation in life.

One of my other long lasting friends was Erica from the Fremont Pawn Shop, Downtown. Erica was Norwegian, in her mid forties and was a typical Nordic stereotype: sparkling ice blue eyes that seemed as big as Lake Mead, long blonde shoulder length hair, slim and elegant in size and demeanour with a flawless North European skin which had not been weathered by the desert sun. If Delta Airlines ever needed a model then Erica would have been the girl for them. She was ex Delta cabin crew who had married a pilot and settled in Las Vegas.

Erica's friendship lasted about five years and she was one of the few friends I made in Vegas that knew both my wives. We first met when my first wife H and I wandered into the 24 hour Pawn Shop just off Fremont Street to view a rather large figurine that was offered for sale. This was in the early days when a European accent was a novelty in Vegas, and Erica recognised the English accent and we spent about 20 or so minutes talking to her whilst she boxed up the figurine for us. Later that day we ran into her in the Fremont coffee shop and that was the start of a friendship that would continue throughout my next 4 or 5 yearly visits to Vegas.

Throughout the years between my two marriages I would visit the pawn shop. These were the years before the common use of personal emails, text messages, Smart phones and WhatsApp etc; so my appearances were always a surprise and were always greeted by a wonderful beaming smile and a warm welcome. We would then

Friends

arrange to meet later at either the Fremont or Binions coffee shop. Over the years she was a sort of Vegas confidant as I would make these visits on my own and we would talk of many things, both personal and political. I must make the point that Erica was happily married and in these liaisons there was nothing sexual or romantic about them, it was just platonic friends from different parts of the world meeting and catching up on each other's news.

Although Erica was perfectly happy in her marriage, I always got the impression that she was not completely happy with Las Vegas and had a rather sad resignation to living in the city. She was very quiet and gave the impression of being somewhat aloof in nature and I don't think that this fitted in well with the rather more American exuberant character. It must have been quite a turnaround for her to go from a Stewardess (old fashioned word) on one of the world's top airlines to working behind the counter in a Vegas pawn shop. These were the days before the mass global communications of Facebook, Twitter, Skype and others that I have no understanding of, and I think she missed her family - especially her sisters and parents. She seemed happy just to talk to another European.

I got the impression that the Pawn Shop manager was a hard task master and it was difficult for Erica to get time off for both visits to Norway and the time off needed when her husband was at home between flights. Despite her quiet reserved nature she said that she did enjoyed working in the shop, meeting and talking to people from different parts of the US and the occasional International visitors. One of my later visits to Vegas and the pawn shop was with my second wife J. J was some 20 years my junior and she and Erica got on very well on the couple of occasions we met in the Fremont coffee shop. One of my lasting memories of the last of those occasions when Erica said to the pair of us:

"Age does not make any difference; I can see that you two are going to make it".

A couple of years later J and I were divorced - you got that one wrong Erica! Little did I know that this would be the last time I saw Erica.

The following year I travelled Downtown from the Strip looking forward to seeing Erica again, but the pawn shop and Erica were gone - replaced by a cheap drinks shop. I hope she is ok.

Another person who although not actually could honestly not really be called a friend but someone who I got into the habit of making a point to visit and chat with over the years. Jake was the manager of the tattoo shop in the Mirage and it was a strange first meeting that led to these yearly UK catch ups. I joined the Navy at the tender age of 17, and it was almost compulsory in those days to get yourself a tattoo - I was no exception, and so on one riotous night of revelry in Portsmouth I festooned myself with a forearm tattoo.

I was wandering around the tattoo shop in the Mirage one afternoon just observing the modern art that now passes for a tattoo, when the assistant came over and said in a Southern English accent:

"Need any help sir?".

"No fine, thank you, just browsing".

We both recognised the common British accent and the usual 'what brings you to Vegas etc.', ensued. Jake had moved from Los Angeles to Vegas around 4 years previously and was in fact manager of the shop.

"So, where did you get the tattoos?", he asked.

"Oh, a long time ago in Portsmouth in the '60's - when I was in the Navy".

"Not under the arches near the Royal Naval Barracks - in the 60's?, he asked.

"Yes, that's the place - do you know it?".

With that Jake waved all the rest of his staff over shouting:

Friends

"Guys, guys, come and look - Goff's work".

Apparently, this Goff was a legend in the tattoo world and he had trained Jake in Portsmouth many, many years ago. So for a couple of minutes that afternoon my forearms caused quite a stir in the Mirage, and although this did not create as much excitement on my subsequent visits to the shop, it was nice to see Jake from time to time and chat about Portsmouth and days gone by.

Another ex UK resident in Vegas who I make a point of visiting every year is Steve who owns the Hat Shop in the Miracle Mile Shops. Steve hails from Essex and has owned and run the shop with his Asian wife for as long as I can remember. I still have a straw boater that I bought from Steve many, many years ago and it has been through the washing machine on numerous occasions. Last time I went and spoke with him I showed him a picture of me wearing the hat with Ann at Wimbledon in the Centre Court seats - I think it made his day; the shop was full of American tourists, so I think it went down well with him. The last time I was talking to him he was thinking about moving his business to San Diego and moving out of Vegas, I will miss chatting to him if he does.

The last person I would like to mention is Ralf who comes from near Frankfurt in Germany. Ralf and I became friends through playing poker in the Excalibur card room. In the later years we would have many friendly discussions about the decision of the British to leave the European Union - Ralf just could not understand it; and in the end it was hopeless for me to try and explain the rationale behind it. We both came at the same time by coincidence when the WSOP was taking place and would travel down to the Rio a couple of times over the two weeks to watch the big games. Ralf was a builder by trade back in Germany but did not play poker at home, the only time he played was when in Vegas. So he really hit it hard and would play all day, through the night and into the early hours of the

Friends

morning until the game broke up usually about 4am in the morning.

On my last visit to Vegas he appeared at the Excalibur card room about 4pm in the afternoon and just having come from the airport, he still had his suitcases with him and had not booked into any hotel. He sat down to play poker, played all night into the next day and then went looking for somewhere to stay. However, when he went to his usual motel, as it was 4th July weekend it was full, so he came back to the Excalibur card room played through the day and into the night and in the morning drove round Vegas looking for a cheap motel to stay for the 2 weeks. He eventually found somewhere and slept for 2 days before appearing again in the Excalibur card room. Poker dedication!

Part IV: Poker

Shuffle up and Deal
Poker, Gambling and Public Perception
Poker Trivia and Quotes
Skill, Luck, Superstition and Rules
Poker Trivia and Quotes
Professionals, Semi Professionals and Amateurs
Poker Trivia and Quotes
Subterfuge, Collusion and Downright Cheating
Beginners at the Table
Final Thoughts

Chapter 1

 Shuffle up and Deal:

This book does not intend to discuss the history of the game of poker, or indeed to explain the rules or theory of Texas Holdem - the main variety of poker played today. Nor is it so conceited in attempting to instruct how to improve your poker game; if I was that good the book would be written from the perspective of a "High Stakes Player". There are many books to aid the novice, from the old school of poker players such as, what some call the bible of poker, Doyle Brunson's *'Super System'*, and also from the top young professionals like Daniel Negreanu's *'Hold'em Wisdom for all Players'*, and Phil Helmouth's *'Play Poker Like the Pros'*.

Suffice to say that its history is clouded in time, and possibly is a form derived from the 16th century Spanish game 'Primero' or the 18th century French game 'Poque' bought to America by the French and subsequently becoming popular in New Orleans and the Southern States of America. The history of poker is just as much about the characters of the past than the mechanics of the game itself. From Wild Bill Hickok, Doc Holliday and Bat Masterton of the Old West, through to Johnny Moss, Doyle Brunson and Amarillo Slim of the 1950's and 60's. It is these unique individuals that added to the mystique of the game, lending themselves to the perception of a life lived by the consequences of the turn of a card. It is the 'life lived on the edge' perception that has led to the game of poker being played by millions in homes, clubs, pubs and now online all over the world. Whatever the history of the game, throughout time is has always consisted of three main elements: cards, money and bluffing, and as noted by Harris in *'Poker & Pop Culture'*: *'........played by cowboys and card sharps; presidents and peasants and by painted dogs'*.

The game has had many changes over the years, but what is not in dispute is that the modern version of Texas Hold'em emerged from the Texas town of Robstown in the early 1900s. It was eventually bought to prominence in the US by the so termed 'Texas Road Gamblers', a variety of characters who made their living by playing poker on the road in various venues around the Southern states of America. It was these road gamblers predominately led by Johnny Moss that bought the game to Las Vegas in the early 1970s at the behest of Moss's old friend Bennie Binion. It was a difficult and dangerous life, as quoted by one of the more famous of them, Amarillo Slim in Des Wilson's book *'Ghosts at the Table'*:

'As a road gambler you had to do four things: Find the game; Beat the game; Not get arrested; Not get robbed'.

Texas Hold'em has been something of a revolution in poker over the last few decades. Rising from obscurity to become the most recognised version of the game throughout the world. It is one of the easiest forms of poker to understand, yet it maintains that incredibly high level of potential mastery for which poker is known. It is the main form of poker that is featured in the highly competitive World Series of Poker.

Throughout this section on poker, and indeed in other sections of the book reference has been made to the World Series of Poker > World Series > WSOP. It is not my intention to go into this premier poker event, as this is a book worth writing on its own. However, I feel it is important for the poker disadvantaged to understand what in fact it represents.

The WSOP is the ultimate proving ground for any poker player, and the Main Event although does not always carry the most prize money, allows the winner to be titled World Champion. It is also the richest sporting event in the world, depending on whether or not you consider poker a sport. The 2018 WSOP attracted a record 123,865 participants from 102 countries, and 2018 marked the fifth consecutive year and sixth overall that the total prize pool eclipsed $200 million.

There are numerous events and different styles of poker held over the 6 week period of the Series with 74 different gold bracelets to be won. The winner of every separate event wins a gold bracelet, plus millions of dollars in prize money. Some of these varied events include: The Ladies Tournament; The Champions Tournament; The Seniors Tournament (50+); The Tag Team (2 - 4 person teams); and The Casino Employees Tournament, plus a multitude of other type of poker games (other than Texas Hold'em) at different financial entry levels.

The Main Event with its $10,000 entry fee is the most recognised poker tournament in the world and winning this event makes the winner not only very rich but a well respected name in the poker world. In fact the WSOP slogan is: 'Where millions are paid and legends are made'. This one event alone stretches over some ten days of play.

This unique poker event was as noted previously introduced by Benny Binion in the 1970's and was held at the Binions Horseshoe Casino on Fremont Street, Downtown, Las Vegas. It is now held at the Rio casino and at the time of writing is allegedly scheduled to move to Caesars Palace in the next couple of years.

It is noted by Karlin as:

'The poker players field of dreams', and the whole six weeks event being like: *'A carnival on steroids'.*

Poker is unique above the majority of sports, games, activities and hobbies in that it is not contaminated by age, social status, background or sex. None of things mean an iota when you are sitting at the table. You are on your own - no team mates to help you out when you make a bad move - no young 25 year old has an advantage over the 75

Shuffle up and Deal

year old - no macho male has an advantage over a quiet, demur female - and no University educated kid with a string of letters after his name is superior to the player who left school at 16 with no qualifications. In 2018 the youngest player in the World Series was 21; the oldest was Jake Ury at 97 - Jake lasted until the third day and received claps and a standing ovations upon exiting the casino.

Their are few incidences in life where a mixture of the above can sit down and play for hundreds, thousands or millions of dollars and all start as equals and all have a reasonable chance of winning. The prospect of winning large amounts of money in the large World Series is the same for the amateur and the professional.

The winner of the 2005 Main Event was a chiropractor turned mortgage broker from Australia named Joe Hachem. Hachem won $7 million for an entry fee of $10,000. In 2003 the Main Event was won by Chris Moneymaker who was an American amateur poker player who won his $10,000 entry fee to the Main Event through a $86 tournament online. It is one of the most famous victories in the history of the World Series as Moneymaker went on to beat a field of 839, many of them professional players winning the gold bracelet and $2.5 million in the process. Moneymaker's win gave hope to millions of other amateur players around the world.

Another aspect of poker that appeals to me personally is that you have control over the outcome, unlike team games you are on your own, the architect of your own destiny. Nobody else sees your cards but yourself except for the showdown, so if you are playing badly only you know and only you knows how to put it right. You can approach each game exactly as you fancy without any regard to a team, and at the start of an evening's poker you can decide: *"Should I put my headphones on and relax listen to my music and have a fun night"*, **or** *"Tonight, no music, concentrate, stick to the plan and maximise my* *winnings"*. You have control over the whole event. As Holden puts it in *'Big Deal'*:

'Poker players like to be their own man, in charge of their own destiny, unreliant on partners, conventions........'

To me this is one of the beauties of playing poker, it is a game and in many cases a living, for the loner. The person who in general likes their own company or perhaps a naturally shy person who is socially inept in crowds or groups. They can learn the game in solitude, they can improve their game by their own analysis and they can play at whatever level suits them in a variety of venues of their own choosing.

When the poker player wakes up in the morning and thinks what happened in the game last night, as I suspect most poker players of all levels do, the discussion will be with themselves. The initial feeling of *"uuggh"*, how much did I lose last night", or, the soft happy feeling of *"how much did I win last night"* will be quickly followed by a self analysis of how either one of the above events occurred. The remedy or continuation of the above situations rests solely with the player himself.

Many books have been written on the psychology of poker and the philosophical view of the game as being a mirror image of life itself. It is an interesting subject but not one I am obliged to enter into in this book. Suffice to say that others have described it well, and the literary critic Al Alvarez notes it well in his introduction to an edition of Yardlye's book *'The Education of a Poker Player'*

'What applied so cogently to money invested in a poker pot applied equally to the feelings I (Alvarez) had invested in my disastrous personal affairs......the only puzzle is why? I should have discovered these in Shakespeare, or Done or Lawrence or Elliot'.

Whilst noting this psychological influence on poker I feel it relevant to mention the identification of 'tells' in poker. For the poker disadvantaged this means the small body movements and language that a player may give that will give some information to the other players on the strength or weakness of their hand. My believe is that it is a word bandied about in the poker fraternity and the poker media, and I have never had a great conviction of its importance in poker. My mitigation is that everyone and his dog knows about 'tells' - so what is to stop a player deliberately displaying this body language to his/her own advantage?

One of the well known phrases in poker is 'showboating' i.e, acting in a certain way to try and disguise your hand usually by taking an inordinate length of time to play, in the hope that your opponents will think you have a difficult decision to make. Any player worth his salt can see this a mile off, and I have seen on many, many occasions when players have tried this and other more experienced players at the table will audibly snore or "*Zzzzzzzzz*" in annoyance.

Rather than rely on these 'tells' I would much rather rely on a player's pattern of play which gives a much more reliable indication of the cards they are holding. It is a well known concept, and two of the world's best Sam Trickett and Daniel Negreano are experts at using this knowledge gained from other players at the table.

Chapter 2

 Poker, Gambling and Public Perception:

Over the years I have made many trips to Vegas to play poker; sometimes profitable, sometimes not; but always enjoyable. The best thing in the world is winning at poker in Vegas, the second-best thing in the world is losing at poker in Vegas.

However, before discussing poker I would like to address a long established debate, that of the difference (if there is one) between playing poker and gambling; ie., can poker be defined as 'gambling'. It very much depends on which dictionary you choose, but most follow the description of the two I have noted below:

US Lexicon Dictionary: *'the act of gambling is an enterprise undertaken or attempted with risk of loss and a chance of success or profit'.*

Cambridge English Dictionary: *'to do something that involves risks that might result in loss of money or failure, hoping to get money or achieve success'* .

If we accept the definitions (and others) as noted above, then yes, poker could be defined as gambling per se. If it is so, then poker if played properly is the most controlled and disciplined manner of gambling. However, this could apply to many aspects of life, and as an example I quote the American billionaire Warren Buffet: Gambling is: *'socially revolting.'* (ITFM 2014). This quote is from a man who made his fortune on betting on the stock market from the age of 11. My perception of these academic definitions are to be taken that if poker is a form of gambling, then many financial dealings that people do in their everyday life can be construed as gambling, but would they define themselves as 'gamblers'?

In her book *'For Richer, For Poorer'* Victoria Coren describes the characteristics of a gambler. She tells the story of poker friend who travelled for seven miles across London to borrow a travel plug adapter from someone at the Vic poker room, thereby (after petrol costs) saving himself about £2. He was in fact later that week travelling to Europe to play poker, where he would be gambling tens of thousands of pounds. Coren had played against him many times. In fact, she had seen him wager £100 plus on the turn of a card, sometimes losing thousands in one sitting. Yet, he had driven for an hour across London to save £2. Gamblers mentality!

Sometimes I see the same characteristics in myself, I have played in poker games for thousands of dollars in Vegas yet will cogitate over the price of one cut of meat a few pence cheaper than another in my local supermarket - gamblers mentality. Whilst playing poker in Vegas I get free meals at the casino buffet and free drinks and I don't pay the dreaded resort fee. So, when I total all these items I am already about $600 up on my two weeks visit before I start playing therefore if I lose $600 on the trip, I have broke even. I have had tried to explain this many times to my friends on return but these mere mortals have difficulty understanding it - gamblers mentality!

In his excellent book *'Gambling for Life'* Frank Findlay describes gambling in these terms:

'If I work hard winning five thousand on a Saturday I feel like a millionaire on the Sunday. When you are a gambler you don't have to be a millionaire to feel like one'

Findlay is a professional gambler who has won and lost millions in his life, and an example of this 'all or nothing' gambling mentality is seen during a precarious time in his life. He had lost everything on a business venture into greyhound racing, and was in the depth of despair; contemplating suicide, never leaving the house for five months, not eating and losing his mansion in an affluent part of the South of England. So, in the summer of 2014 in consultation with his wife, he sold his old car for £6,000 a watch for £5,000; placed £2,000 on a horse which won netting him another £5,000. He then gambled the total of £16,000 on the 2014 World Cup in Brazil and turned it into £72,000. Only a true gambler would contemplate such a perilous course of action.

There are of course poker players who are compulsive gamblers too; the aforementioned Stu Unger is an obvious example; a great poker player but a degenerate gambler - it was gambling that led to the sad and depressing end of his life - not poker.

I have seen many of these people in my life, some are good poker players and bad gamblers, some have been very good disciplined gamblers but bad poker players - very rarely have I witnessed someone who is good at both!

One of the big differences between a gambler and a poker player is that a gambler is prone to taking much greater risks than a good poker player. Although both risks are dependent on mathematical odds and probabilities, the poker player will usually leave himself with 'outs' i.e, the way he can minimise or maximise the chances of his hand winning the pot, a gambler rarely does. The poker player also has to make decisions during the game; they may be the right ones, or the wrong ones, but he/she does have a choice. The gambler has no choice once he has place his bet, whether it be on a roulette wheel, a horse race or a football game.

Gamblers also tend to be risk takers in the life in general, and possibly see themselves as more exciting than others who prefer security in their lives and relationships. There are of course many poker players who will show the same traits in their personal life; as noted in the 'Early Years' Chapter which remarks on players who went to live abroad to play poker. I will mention here a Norwegian player I met in Vegas a few years ago. He was an accomplished player who played in higher stake games than myself, and was in Vegas for the World Series. I had breakfast with him a couple of times in the Excalibur and he told me that he moved from his home in Norway to live and play poker in Malta.

However, I have found that in general it is the high stakes players who make this type of life changing move, usually to be nearer 'the action'. Low stakes players such as myself usually manage to keep their personal life risk factor to a minimum in regards to their poker playing. Holden makes one simple but excellent difference between poker players and gamblers that he describes as crucial:

'A gambler, be he one who bets on horses or sports events, on casino games or raindrops running down a window pane, is someone who wages unfavourable odds. A poker player, if he knows what he is doing, wages favourable odds - one is a romantic, the other a realist'.

Some similarities of both poker players and gamblers can be seen in the marked difference between amateurs and professionals. Both professional gamblers and professional poker players are just like the successful businessmen. They are committed to their jobs and responsibilities, are disciplined in planning and executing their strategies, and can handle the highs and lows that the system creates.

In a 2013 study by Weinstock of Saint Louis University *'Professional and Pathological Gamblers: Similarities and Differences',* it was found that the professionals gambled or played poker for about 70% during any three month period. They also considered it serious work and had the ability to control their behaviour without emotional feelings of 'excitement, thrills or a buzz' etc., as the reason for gambling. The study also confirmed that successful poker players and gamblers usually had high IQs, averaging 125, and virtually none of the professionals ever buy lottery tickets.

Many scholarly studies have been done around, but not exactly focused on the differences and similarities, of poker playing and gambling addiction, and two are noted here:

'Differences between Poker Players and Non-Poker-Playing Gamblers'

This research conducted amongst American University Students concluded that poker players were more likely to develop into problem gamblers than non-poker players, leading to problem and addictive gambling. (Shead et al 2008)

'Problem gambling in poker: money, rationality and control in a skill-based social game'

This research was conducted between two sets of respondents: 14 poker playing addictive gamblers, and 15 professional/recreational poker players. The research demonstrated the distinction between poker and other forms of gambling games, with poker identified as a skill based game. However, it did identify that poker has implications for the way that problem gambling can arise in poker players (Ole Bjerg 2010).

Both these studies agree that playing poker can lead to gambling, and perhaps in time, to compulsive gambling. In consequence, it possibly shows that there are certain similarities between poker players and gamblers. However, whether or not this shows that poker players are gamblers or not, is still open to debate and is perhaps left to the perception of the player themselves.

In other research into slot machine gambling in the USA Natasha Dow notes in her book *'Addiction by Design: Machine Gambling in Las Vegas'* that most gamblers at an AA meeting she attended stated that:

Poker, Gambling and Public Perception

'Gambling as I see it, is an irrational behaviour that is impulsive'.

A gambling addiction is of course a serious matter, and I do not wish to make light of a person's destructive habit, but I have never heard of a 'Poker Players Anonymous', or that someone playing continuous sessions of poker can be described as having an 'illness' or a 'disorder'. The sad thing is that the recognition of this 'illness' is not recognised by the addict until it is too late, and the damage to themselves and their family has been done. As stated in Chapter 1, I learned this early on in my poker life and since then have never played poker because I **have** to win, only because I **want** to win.

Another perception of the good or evil can be seen in the way that regulating authorities in different parts of the world allow, or don't allow poker or gambling.

In the USA poker is allowed in most states, as is gambling. However, American citizens are not allowed to play poker online in certain states, but can gamble online. The regulations re gambling in the USA are chaotic and seem to have no logic attached to them. There are no legal casinos in Tennessee, but have a state lottery; Mississippi have legal casinos, but no state lottery. Casinos are illegal in many other USA states: Kentucky, South Carolina, Virginia, Vermont to name a few. The state of Utah prohibits any form of gambling. Designated Native American reserves can have casinos whichever state they are in.

The law in the UK is somewhat different, in that it is not the number of casinos that is regulated, but regulates the gambling opportunities in those casinos.

I really don't see myself as a gambler, just a poker player - and I believe that many poker players I have come across over the years think that way too. I believe that poker can best be described as a game with a brilliant combination of strategy, maths, psychology and sprinkled with a hint of chance.

Poker, Gambling and Public Perception

There are fundamental differences between gamblers and poker players, and also some similarities. The main similarities are that of money management and self discipline. In fact money management is an essential element in poker trips to Las Vegas, the last thing anyone wants is to run out of available money in the first two days in Vegas. I can think of no other form of torture so abhorrent than being a gambler in Vegas with no money! Of course all casinos in Vegas circumnavigate this likely problem by placing cash point machines at strategic places throughout the casino.

I tend to manage poker money on a day to day basis when playing in Vegas, rather than a weekly or fortnightly basis. For example; if I am losing during any particular part of the day I do not put a financial ceiling on my losses, and I do not stop playing until the end of the day. However, I do not play the next day - thereby equalling out my expenses on my daily allowance. Sometimes, this takes a remarkable measure of discipline and I usually use such times to take in the other advantages of Vegas; sunbathing, sightseeing, watching the bigger poker tournaments etc.

One of the other things that I believe is difficult for the poker disadvantaged to understand that to be successful at poker you need to have a total disregard to money. The poker player becomes accustomed to putting the monetary value of the chips in front of them out of their mind. It is no use thinking:

"What could I have bought with that?", or *"How many hours did I have to work to make that?"*.

It goes back to my earlier comment, do not play with money you cannot afford to lose. If you are doing this, then you should not be playing.

The aforementioned Stu Unger had absolutely no concept of monetary value. Like the gambler mentioned by Victoria Coren, he would count of $100 bills at a betting window without thought of their value, but all his clothes were bought second hand. When the car he was driving broke down, he would simply leave it in the street and buy another one. He would present a $100 bill for a $1.50 cup of coffee and could not understand why the vender was annoyed. As mentioned he died practically penniless, without any assets, bank account or fixed address.

Whilst I am not suggesting that new poker players adopt this general attitude towards money, but it is important to separate monetary value from the chips in front of them. The value of chips has no equation to the amount in the real world. It is essential to keep in touch with both of the worlds - the real and the poker worlds - so a reckless disregard for money does not develop and the social player finds themselves completely out of their depth and plays above their bankroll.

I think it is also important to note the difference between social players, who are predominately low stakes players and social players who are also gamblers in other areas. The social player usually has a stable way of life with a situation that shows maturity and his/her life style balance means that poker can remain a hobby and does not cause problems in respect to his family or professional life. The social player has a clear financial limit that ensures they are never in any financial danger, with perhaps a 'poker budget' that is disconnected from the necessities of life. Their objective is to master the game's complexities and techniques not to make money.

If this social player also has a gambling addiction their lack of life balance leads them to put more importance on poker as a form of gambling and there is a hazy financial situation with money that is required for these life essentials being used to play poker and to gamble in general. Money then becomes the primary motivation for playing the game with a fantasy view of the game solving all their problems in life.

Poker Trivia and Quotes

The French introduced the suits in playing cards we know today, and they represent four classes of men. Spades stands for Nobility, Diamonds stands for Merchants, Clubs stands for Peasants and Hearts stands for Clergy.

The most difficult aspects of playing poker professionally are coping emotionally with the losses and coping with the recurring idea that you're not doing anything worthwhile.
~ Mike Caro

Pro poker player Tom Dwan started playing online poker with the $50 his dad gave him for his birthday and earned over $5,000,000 in the next 3-4 years.

Andrei Karpov was so desperate to stay in a poker game in 2007 he put his wife up as a stake after he'd run out of money. He then lost. She was so angry she left him for the winner Sergey Brodov.

You can't play Texas Hold'em in Texas. Poker rooms are essentially illegal in Texas, with the exception of one casino on an Indian reservation and this card room that found a loophole.

The biggest amount won in the Main Event at the WSOP was $12 million by Jamie Gold in 2006.

Poker, Gambling and Public Perception

I have a few 'discussions' over the years with people, especially people from my church who consider my poker and visits to Las Vegas as a sin, and that I should be prayed for.

I remember with affection the first time I went to my church house group. I thought; *"I had better get it out from the start"*, so told them apart from my real job as a Prison Officer, I also played poker and made a couple of trips to Las Vegas every year.

"Never mind Mike", said John, the house bible group leader, *"We will pray for you"*.

Of course, John, an ex policeman, assumed in all good faith that I was a degenerate gambler who needed saving from the devil and this addictive sin. But of course, in my mind I am thinking *"What John, are you going to pray that I hit a full house on the flop and everyone at the table is betting into me?"*. John and his wife Bett are genuinely nice people and good Christians, so I smiled and said:

"Thank you John; please do"

I have over the years defended my poker (and gambling if you must call it that), by pointing out that investing in stocks and shares, premium bonds or an ISA is no different. You are laying down money in the hope of getting more than you 'bet' in return, with the risk of losing some or all of the money you have invested. No different; in fact I go on to explain that at least in a game of poker I have some sort of control over the money I have invested, I have the control over whether I win or lose by using my skill and knowledge of the game. But once you give your money to the Fund Manager, Building Society or to the Treasury, you have no control over it, it is out of your hands and you are at the mercy of the stock market or the computer known as 'Ernie'. Therefore, it is a bigger gamble than my poker play.

Dostoyevsky made a similar comment many years ago in his 1866 book *'The Gambler'*

'And why should gambling be worse than any other means of making money – for instance, commerce? It is true that only one out of a hundred wins, but what is that to me?'.

I would like to conclude this section by quoting from the abstract of an article from the Journal of Gambling Issues in 2013 by Gaelle Boujul *et al:*

'The authors examined gamblers' perceptions of Texas Hold'Em (HE) poker..... Sixteen regular HE gamblers were assessed through a semi-structured interview and took part in a session of gambling exposure....... Problem gamblers had an emotional profile that was characterized by a lack of self-regulation and difficulties with delayed gratification........ and the results support the fact that poker deserves to be set apart from other gambling forms, especially when it comes to prevention and treatment'.

The research by Boujul is both valid and reliable and for anyone interested in a more academic approach to the issue of poker with its associate skills and gambling it is worth reading.

This perception by the general public of poker and poker players as noted in the above regarding my house group leader is an interesting issue. I think that the more poker comes into the general knowledge and understanding of people by films such as 'Rounders', or TV coverage of the World Series and the World Poker Tour the more the perception by the population is changing for the better. This public perception is perhaps not quite as bad in the US as the game is more widely played in homes and by families - more on the level of a family Saturday night event than a gambling addiction. Many people who are against gambling in any form and see it as decadent will never accept poker as long as it is played in casinos - which themselves are sinful and immoral. So perhaps it is this location of a game that colours a person' image of poker and poker players, and it

Poker, Gambling and Public Perception

will always be lumped together with other gambling games such as roulette or craps.

It is hard to say with any certainty where someone gets their ideas from regarding poker and poker players. I think that this synonymy of poker and gambling is prevalent and perhaps the fact that poker is played for money, whereas Rummy or Whist is not. I have a friend with whom I would play tennis who also ran a weekly Whist game, and whenever I mentioned poker, she would screw up her face with distaste as if I had mentioned the underworld and the very devil himself. She considered poker as perhaps the lowest form of any card game, and trying to persuade her that it contained elements of skill and strategy was a complete waste of time - it was gambling pure and simple.

I think there has also been a different perspective from the public's misunderstanding with the realization that part skill plays in poker. Also, that being good at poker needs a reasonable understanding of maths, strategy and psychology coupled with the interviews on TV of intelligent young men and women with University degrees, poker is slowing losing its shady, back room reputation.   Poker players and the authorities are in a continual battle with law making bodies to get poker exempt from gambling laws, and to get the legal identity of a 'game of skill'

Then of course there is the image of the poker player in opposition to other high earners in life. On one side we have the image of the rich young stock broker or hedge fund manager: in a suit, carrying a brief case, clean shaven and eating lunch in expensive delis. The rich young poker player wanders into the Bellegio or Wynns card room, in trainers, track suit bottoms, hoodie, scruffy and unshaven - believe me reader I have seen them, day after day. Both make large amounts of money in their daily grind, both gamble (the poker player with his own money, the trader with other people's) - but the public perception of the first is that of a successful young business man, the type you

Poker, Gambling and Public Perception

would love your daughter to marry - the second is a degenerate gambler who you would not let near your daughter with a barge pole. This public perception even encroaches on language and discourse in the form of idiom, phrases and metaphor that are used in everyday life that originate from the game of poker:

'When the chips are down';   *'The buck stops here';*

'Put your cards on the table';   *'A poker face';*

'It is not what you are dealt, but how you play it';   *'Up the anti';*

'Running bad>Running hot';   *'Raise the stakes';*

Chapter 3

 Skill, Luck, Superstition and Rules:

I think that there is little doubt that poker is the most popular card game in the world. Everyday hundreds and thousands of people play poker for real money on the internet. This book does not intend to discuss or analyse the positives or negatives of online poker, but just to give an example of the popularity of the game. In 2013 online poker rooms generated approximately £2.8 billion in gross wins (H2 Gambling Capital).

It is worth noting however that the brakes were put on this internet explosion when in September 2006 the US senate passed the 'Unlawful Internet Gambling Enforcement Act' - it passed into law and was signed by George W Bush within a fortnight. The Act did not make online poker illegal, but it made the transfer of money between online gambling sites and banks, credit card companies etc illegal. This made it virtually impossible to play poker online in the USA. The poker authorities have been trying ever since to get this changed, mainly by the route of establishing poker as a game of skill, therefore declaring the poker sites as non gambling. The fight is ongoing!

At the same time there is widespread controversy over the legality of poker in relation to taxation of the winnings of poker players, online or in live games. A key issue in this discussion is again whether poker can be considered a game of skill or luck. Many countries across the world have separate taxes for 'gambling and games of chance', whilst money won in a game of skill are usually subject to the countries regular income tax laws and in countries such

Skill, Luck, Superstition and Rules

as the USA there is also a great variation from state to state.

It is always open to debate whether or not poker is a game of skill, or just dependant on luck. In his book *'The Mammoth Book of Poker'*, Paul Mendelson believes that it is about 5% skill and 95% luck. I am not quite sure I agree with this, and would put the 'skill' factor slightly higher at perhaps 15%. He also notes that

'At the end of the day, cards is cards, and poker is gambling'.

I not sure that I agree with this either, it is too much of an in general statement and it is imprecise to lump all card games under one heading.

Whatever the percentage there can be no doubt that luck has a critical role to play in poker, both in its seen percentage of the game and the players ability to cope with it. It is not like other sports such as chess, darts, tennis etc., where skill is the main factor to success. The amateur can sit down with the skilled professional and win if good luck and bad look is playing its corresponding part in the game. This is what makes the game of poker so inviting in that luck can overcome skill in the short run.

There have been many classic examples of this over the years at the World Series as noted above, but one I witnessed in 2017 was the now famous run of the British amateur John Hesp. Although John was not a rank amateur he had no business making the final table of the World Series, finishing fourth out of thousands of players and netted himself some $2.6 million in the process by shear good luck and some very competent and skilful moves on his part. John is a 60 year grandfather from East Yorkshire in the UK, and had never won anything more than a couple of thousand pounds in his local casino poker game. He came to Vegas on a dream, dressed the part in a colourful, loud jacket with matching shirt and a straw hat and with a determination to enjoy himself and follow his dream.

Skill, Luck, Superstition and Rules

It is however not only this combination of luck and carefully used skill that made John famous - his story led to interviews on both UK and USA television, and articles dedicated to him in such eminent papers as the San Francisco Times, the Las Vegas Journal and the US Today, as well as some British Press - it was the nature of his success. Hesp added a different flavour to the biggest poker tournament of the year, entertaining players and spectators alike with his banter and table chat. The young, dour faced uncommunicative professionals at that final table had never witnessed anything like Hesp - they just did not know how to handle him or his play. He was recognised throughout the poker fraternity as a shot in the arm - just what poker needed to change its gloomy, depressing face.

After being knocked out of the tournament Hesp said this in an interview to the Las Vegas press:

'I've absolutely loved it, and I just hope that I've spread a little light, happiness, and fun into the game. I'm told that there's a lot of people watching that have never watched it before, so that's good for the TV ratings, and I think that people do like fun'.

'I just hope that I've given you people entertainment, and pleasure in the way I've been playing. If I've done anything in my life, it's that I've shown that this game doesn't have to be boring, people can have fun'.

However, when it comes to luck poker players are some of the most delusional people in the world. For every mistake we make at the poker table there is always a rational way to explain it - if only this card had come or not come on the river - if only that maniac in the early position had not raised - if only that buffoon had not slowed played his aces etc., - and then when everything else fails we can always blame sheer bad luck:

'Is it really not possible to touch the gaming table without being instantly infected by superstition?' - Fyodor Dostoyevsky

Skill, Luck, Superstition and Rules

The above quote from Dostoyevsky book *'The Gambler'* brings me on to another element that seems to prevail amongst a certain number of poker players amateur and professionals alike, that of superstition. It maybe superstition regarding clothing worn, trinkets and icons that they take to the table, cards they like or dislike - the combinations of these false notion are never ending and I would challenge any honest poker player to deny its existence in some form or other.

Walk into any busy poker room and there will always be a few players that are using their own trinket or token to cover their cards or place on top of their stack of chips. Usually a small figurine or a poker chip from another casino, but whichever it is these items are significant to the particular player.

It is odd that poker players will spend half their playing lives explaining to others that they do not appreciate the contribution that lady luck may make to their game; and then spend the other half balancing a lucky token or rabbits foot on their chips. This is after they have requested that the card room manager or the dealer place them in their 'lucky' number one, three, six........ seat.

It is not only physical entities that poker players will depend on to give their play that little bit of extra edge. Discourse, phrases and general poker idioms can also be heard in card rooms around the world. It would be unusually to spend an evening in a poker room without hearing the shout of *'just one time'* from a player who is hoping for that lucky card to beat all the odds that will fall and save him from losing the hand.

It is not only small stakes players such as myself use this perceived additional tool of luck to enhance our game. Perhaps the most famous 'token user' is two times World Champion Johnny Chan, nicknamed The Orient Express. Chan can always be seen with a 'lucky' orange at the side of his chips at the poker table. When Chan started his poker career in Vegas he would bring along an orange

Skill, Luck, Superstition and Rules

which would give of a sweet fragrance to over ride the stale odour from the other player's cigarette smoke. Johnny Chan's orange is so legendary in the poker world that in the poker film *'Rounders'* starring Matt Damon and Ed Norton, Chan makes a cameo appearance complete with his 'lucky' orange in one of the poker scenes.

Another legend of poker, the Granddaddy of them all Doyle Brunson even has his own superstition. The legendary Doyle 'Texas Dolly' Brunson wrote in his book *'How I made a $1,000,000 Playing Poker'*:

'I don't eat peanuts at the card table. There's no reason in the world eating peanuts should affect the outcome of the game, but it doesn't cost me anything to observe the taboo against it'.

Many poker players high or low stakes will deny that they rely entirely on luck and insist it is skill that will see them through yet many will have some type of lucky charm; chanted rituals, wearing a particular item of clothing, or some type of superstitious behavioural pattern that they observe either before or during the game.

Poker superstitions are not confined to the influence of outside elements, the actual cards dealt or used can have an unfounded effect upon the players. One of the most irrational request from players I have heard over the 30 years of poker, is for the dealer to change the deck. *What?* - how is this going to affect the action - there are the same 52 cards in each deck - but some player having a bad run of cards thinks this will 'change his luck'. The second most groundless request is for the dealer to give the cards 'a wash'. To the poker disadvantaged this means to shuffle the deck by splashing the cards on the table and mixing the cards by hand - or washing - the cards, rather than a traditional shuffle. *What?* - how is this going to manipulate the order of the cards in their favour?

It is not only the lower stakes players who sometimes succumb to the baseless assumption that certain cards are particularly lucky for them and should be played against all probabilities of poker logic and theory. These players will attach enormous superstition value to certain cards. In an article in The Observer in 2002, Victoria Coren admitted:

'For my part, I'm superstitious about a particular Hold'em hand. There are two weakish cards in the deck which most players will throw away, but if I find them I always raise'.

Coren of course in the true tradition of poker players does not disclose which two cards these are!

I include myself as a reluctant participant in this superstitious ritual - wherever or whatever game I am playing in I will always play the first hand irrespective of my hole cards unless there has been a large raise previous to my turn to act.

I must also admitted for a penchant for a certain starting hand. During my early days of playing in Vegas I was dealt the *6h and 7h* as my hole cards whilst playing in the Plaza poker room. The flop came down *5h; 8h; 9h* - giving me a straight flush. The turn revealed an inconsequential *4c*; and then unbelievably the river produced the *10h* giving me an even higher straight flush. The odds of a straight flush in any hand of Texas Hold'em is around 4,900 to 1 and the odds of hitting a straight flush on the flop are even less; poker equity calculators do not even show the precise odds. Obvious to say that on this occasion I won the pot. What is even more remarkable is that the very next hand I was dealt the 6h and 7h again as my hole cards. I can't even start to work out the odds of that happening, and doubt that it can be, even by the most adept at working out gambling odds.

I of course, held my breath and dared to believe that lady luck could be with me on two consecutive hands. Alas, it did not happen, she deserted me - but what it did do was to consign me to playing those two cards on every occasion they were dealt as my hole cards. This slavery to luck last a good number of years until my poker experience attained a little more sophistication, but even now, every now and then, I am tempted.

These superstitions amongst modern day players are nothing new, and throughout the centuries poker players have always paid regard to them. One of them is epitomised the song by the late Kenny Rogers *'The Gambler'* :

'Never count you chips whilst sitting at the table'.

Another rather more obscure one from the wild west is that:

'Disaster is bound to occur if you play poker with a one-eyed player at the table'.

I will conclude the observations above on superstition in poker with this well known quote:

'Depend on the rabbit's foot if you will, but remember it didn't work for the rabbit.' ~ R. E. Shay

I would agree more with the explanation given by Matthew Parvis of Poker News that poker is:

'A game with a brilliant combination of strategy, maths, psychology sprinkled with a hint of chance'.

Although I would agree with the other components of this description I think the 'sprinkling of chance' is a little over generous!

Luck is synonymous with the edge that a casino has over the players at any of the casino games. The casino will always have the slight edge on the following popular casino games:

- ❖ Blackjack 0.5% if the player plays basic strategy and depending on the number of decks used;
- ❖ Roulette 5.26% with double zero, 2.5% with single zero;
- ❖ Slots 2% - 10%;
- ❖ Craps 1.4% - 5% depending on the bet.

(source: www.Gambling.com)

As noted the casinos in Las Vegas take an average of $650,000 per day, and they do this with the above small

Skill, Luck, Superstition and Rules

advantage percentages. It therefore must compare with a skilled poker player against a non skilled or beginner in a game of Texas Holdem in that the small edge in skill will in the long term ensure financial success against less skilled players irrespective of luck.

Skill, Luck, Superstition and Rules

Poker Trivia and Quotes

"*Poker is a combination of luck and skill. People think mastering the skill part is hard, but they're wrong. The trick to poker is mastering the luck.*" ~ *Jesse May.*

"*Most of the money you'll win at poker comes not from the brilliance of your own play, but from the ineptitude of your opponents.*" ~ *Lou Krieger.*

"*Poker is generally thought to be America's second most popular after-dark activity. Sex is good, they say, but poker lasts longer.*" ~ *Al Alvarez.*

"*Dogs are lousy poker players. When they get a good hand, they wag their tails.*" ~ *Unknown.*

"*You will show your poker greatness by the hands you fold. Not the hands you play*" ~ *Dan Reed.*

"*Last night I stayed up late playing poker with Tarot cards. I got a full house and four people died.*" ~ *Steven Wright.*

"*If I lose today, I can look forward to winning tomorrow, and if I win today, I can expect to lose tomorrow. A sure thing is no fun.*" ~ *Chico Marx.*

Skill, Luck, Superstition and Rules

Every poker player will at some time be cheated by luck - all his/her hard work in learning the game, all the books read, care and dedication to methods of play as been ruined by 'lady luck'. The seasoned player knows this, but it important for the beginner to remember that however despondent in may make you in the short run, it will by the very nature of the entity change, and one sunny, glorious day it will return and revitalize your flagging spirits. I know - I have been there. When these horrifying instances of bad luck strike the only thing I can say to the beginner is to have a silent rant, play the victim, move on and forget the hand as soon as possible. The last thing you want is to be still disturbed by it the next day or the next time you sit down to play.

I urge the player who is stuck in this variance period of back luck to perhaps look at the mathematical theory of 'random walk' which is a very complicated mathematical theory but in simple terms it means the past movement of an entity cannot be used to predict its future. For example: if I tossed a coin it has a 50/50 chance of coming down heads or tails; so would anyone bet that it comes down 95 times heads and 5 times tails? Why not? - it has an equal chance at every toss. The same can be said for a roulette wheel - would anyone bet that the red (against the black) would come up 19 out of every 20 spins? This is of course the law of averages, but the longer the coins comes down heads, or the roulette ball drops in the red sector then more is the chance of the opposite coming up.

Hence, the longer your run of back luck goes on, the better the chance is that it will end soon. So, be patient, stick it out, try not to lose too much money and 'stay calm and carry on'.

I will finish this discussion on skill versus luck by noting that if luck was predominate in poker then there would not be any successful players who are consistently winners in the top games around the world. Everyone would win about the same number of tournaments as the

Skill, Luck, Superstition and Rules

others, as happens in slots, blackjack or craps tournaments. Over the years the records show that skill is a big influence in winning poker.

I would like to digress a little at this point of the discussion on luck and mention a few incidences where only one has relevance to poker. The question is that of Karma - coincidence. I am a believer in Karma, and what happens at every turn can change a life. Everyone can tell a story of coincidence in their live; so here is three of mine which stretches coincidence to the limit.

(a) My father was in the Royal Navy during World War II and his ship was torpedoed and sunk in the Mediterranean. He was adrift in a life boat for 7 days before being picked up and taken as a prisoner of war by the Italian Navy. Some 25 years later my father came to visit me whilst I was also in the Royal Navy stationed at Portsmouth. We went to a pub one Saturday night - my father sat down facing the door - after 5 minutes a gentleman opened the door - looked in, turned round and left. My father ran after him - it was the Coxswain who had been in charge of that life boat in the Mediterranean.

(b) Whilst in the Navy I was onboard HMS Belfast (now moored in the Thames) and worked with a guy for 3 years. Eventually he was drafted and I was drafted to a ship stationed at Singapore. On one of the many Far East exercises we visited Auckland in New Zealand. I walked into a pub in the city centre one night, only to find sitting at the first table through the door, my friend from the Belfast who was on another ship on the exercise.

(c) A poker coincidence. In my early Blackpool years I would pick up another player named Barry who could not drive, and take him to the game. This lasted for about 4 years before we eventually lost touch and I did not see him for around 5 years. One Sunday afternoon I was sitting in seat number 5 waiting for the game to start in the Mirage in Las Vegas. A voice said to me from behind me: *"Excuse me, is this seat number six?"*. I turned round to answer and it was Barry, not only was he in Vegas the same time and in the same game, but had been seated next to me!

Karma, we all experience it at some time in life.

It is hard to explain to the poker disadvantaged that poker is also a game with strict conventions of etiquette, and any deviation from these customs will invoke anger from both the dealer and the other players. It seems strange that a game that consists of bluffing and misleading your opponents can also contain elements of truth and honesty. This is not a book commenting on the 'rules of poker' - as there are no official rules to the game, and for many years this proved a problem for players, dealers and casinos in general. Every country and every casino within that country would have varying rules for the game - it was a nightmare for players such as myself who like to play in as many different card rooms as possible.

The International Poker Federation was launched in April 2009 in Lausanne, Switzerland, home of the Olympic movement and most other sports federations, IFMP champions poker as 'a mind-sport of strategic skill', alongside chess, bridge, draughts and Go with Anthony Holden as its first president.

However, it seems that this organisation was to: campaign to clean up poker's image, to lobby legislators to separate poker from gambling and help to make an international case for poker as a 'mind-sport amongst other things. This is an excellent organisation helping to further poker as an acceptable game which should be separated from gambling, but as far as I can see they did not attempt to devise a 'rule book' for the game. Considering the widespread deviations of the forms of poker and different poker arenas I can fully understand this, it would have been nigh impossible. In all honesty I could not imagine the poker room managers in Vegas

Skill, Luck, Superstition and Rules

imposing a set of rules on their players that had been established in Lausanne, Switzerland. I would suspect (without any belittling) that the majority of them has never heard of Lausanne.

This problem of rules and conventions has now been alleviated by all casinos and card rooms adopting the rules and conventions that are in play during the World Series of Poker. Although not ideal, the situation is far better than existed before. Before any tournament in Las Vegas the card room manager will always without fail read the rules and conventions that operate in that poker room. These rules vary very slightly and in general do not cause any problems for the first time player who knows the general guidelines for tournament play. In cash games, or ring games as they are sometimes called, any questions or queries on the rules of the particular casino or the card room can be explained and dealt with by the dealers.

Some of these fundamentals of good manners and etiquette noted above include things such as: not betting out of turn; not discussing a hand you are not involved in; criticise another players play at the table. Another unwritten 'rule' is that there are two things not to be discussed at a poker table: politics and religion! It is also bad form to 'slowroll'. This involves the showdown i.e., the last two players left in the hand who are required to show their hands. If a player holds an obvious winner and despite whatever his opponent may hold is irrelevant, if this player turns his cards over slowly, or refuses to show until his opponent does so first, or turns his two cards over one at a time - this is called 'slowrolling' and will be seen as disrespectful to the other player.

Only once in my 30 years of playing poker in Vegas have I seen a lapse in this unspoken rule of politics talk at the table. Whilst playing in a tournament in the Mirage a debate started re the US government's attitude towards drugs and so called recreational drugs in particular. I of course kept out of this debate, but as the time went on

Skill, Luck, Superstition and Rules

could see which way it was going - so was even more determined to keep my mouth firmly shut. As the debate got more vociferous the atmosphere around the table got unpleasant and many of the other players dropped out of the debate - like me they saw which way it was going. It continued until there were only two male players left engaged in this - what had now come a dispute. The dealer tried to calm things down, but to no avail. Suddenly one of the men stood up, picked up his stack of chips, threw them across the table at the other player, and shouted: *"F......g government, F........g idiots"* - and stormed out of the card room. The table sat in silence, and I think that those who had been initially involved in the discussion were slightly embarrassed. A lesson learnt.

A good example of poker respect as being different from gambling propriety (if there is one) can be seen in the well reported incident regarding one of the world's top poker players Phil Ivey. Ivey is also a high stakes blackjack player and general gambler and won some £7.7 million at Crockfords Casino playing Baccarat on a visit to London in 2012. Ivey and a colleague, Cheung Yin Sun had noticed that the cards used at Crockfords had been misprinted, and in fact certain cards could be identified from their edges and patterns on the back of the cards. They used this to their advantage and in the following court case stated they were not cheating, just merely using an advantage given by Crockfords' blunder and did not constitute dishonesty.

Ivey subsequently lost the case in the UK High Court who judged in favour of Crockfords, stating that Punto Banco should be a game of chance with neither the player or the casino manipulating the odds in their favour.

The question is: if Phil Ivey had been playing in a high stakes poker game and he had noticed a mark on the back of one of the cards, would he have used this to his advantage and said nothing to the dealer or other players? I obviously cannot say with 100% certainty, but I doubt this very much. I am reasonably confident in saying that any poker player, low or high stakes would have informed the table.

I believe this is an example of a poker player's responsibility to the other players in the game, in opposition to the gambler who has no responsibility to the object or person of the bet, and also how much importance poker players place on these conventions and etiquette at the table.

A further example of poker players being a separate entity to gamblers in general can be seen by the number of well known, and rich, celebrities who are prominent in the poker arena. These superstars play for the love of the game, not the money and frequently give all their winnings to charity. The numbers are too great to list here, but the following is just an account of some of the better known.

Don Cheadle - the American film actor known in poker circles as an active enthusiast of the game and co-founder of the Ante Up for Africa foundation. Cheadle, known for his roles in the Oceans movie series and other blockbusters, founded the "Ante Up for Africa" charity foundation with Annie Duke and Norman Epstein. In terms of a poker player, Cheadle is a very good poker player, and has played in many televised poker tournaments. In 2007 he beat good friend and Full Tilt Pro Phil Ivey at the NBC Heads Up Championship event, and in 2008 he beat David Pham another high stakes poker player. He has also participated in Poker After Dark and Celebrity Poker Shoot Out.

Matt Damon - the American film actor known for his roles in the Jason Bourne trilogies, and for the poker related movie Rounders. Damon is not rated as high as other celebrities on the poker circuit, but is renowned for his charity poker tournaments. As recent as April 2020 Damon and Ben Affleck, another highly rated poker player, held a charity online tournament, with the proceeds of $1.7 million going to 'Feeding America' a non-profit organisation distributing food to those in need amid the outbreak of Covid-19.

Ronaldo Luís Nazário de Lima - one of the best soccer players to ever come out of Brazil and was a member of the World Cup winning Brazilian team of 2002. Ronaldo is frequently seen on the poker circuit, and although not the best of the ranked celebrities, can hold his own in most poker company. He is a member of the Poker Stars Team and can regularly been seen playing online.

Michael Phelps - Olympic swimmer and 18 times gold medal winner. Phelps plays regular on the poker circuit and at the Wynn in Las Vegas, and has also taken part in the World Series of Poker. Phelps is recognised amongst the professional pokers as a good poker player who takes the game seriously. and often takes part in charity events. He is also another great contributor to poker charity events and was instrumental in working with Hollywood actor Josh Brolin in hosting the Big Game Party; an event for 160 players with a buy in of $2,000. The proceeds from the event going to the Giving Back Fund a national charity to support underrepresented groups in their communities.

Toby Maguire (Spiderman) - Maguire played in super high buy-in card games in Hollywood for years, and these games became the basis for the movie *'Molly's Game'*. According to all accounts Maguire was the best player around at the time by a large margin. In addition to this he has made at least three deep runs in the WSOP events which shows he is more than capable of holding his own against the best professionals in the poker world. Maguire was also involved in the 'Feeding America' charity event noted above.

One other rich charity giving poker player is Bill Klien. Klien is a retired business man who sold his company after being diagnosed with throat cancer. He has survived for more than a decade now spends his time playing poker and golf.

Klien is a good poker player who wins a lot of money in tournaments throughout the US. His ethos is simple: anything he wins goes to charity, and this can be best illustrated by this statement he made at the $111,111 buy in event at the WSOP:

'I'm playing in the One Drop event for two charities - the Cystic Fibrosis Foundation and the She Therapeutic Riding Centre. Anything I win I give all to charity. If I don't cash, then I will match my buy-in and give that to charity'.

I have seen Klien play in Las Vegas on many occasions, and although I have never spoken to him, his persona at the poker table indicates the type of man he is. Quiet, never gets into debates or arguments at the table, just plays his game; shrugging when he loses, smiling when he wins and chats amiably to all the other players. One of the best adverts for the game of poker I have ever witnessed.

There are many other well known personalities of the same ilk as Klein, Bill Perkins, David Einhorn, John Morgan - all millionaire business men. It could of course be argued that they could just give the money to charity anyway, but my rationale is to make the point that they give through the medium of an activity they love.

Many of these charitable players are business men and investment analysts and they will maintain it is the same analytical thinking and self-confidence that helps them to win at poker. By playing poker for charity, they debunk the perception of hard hearted business men and move back into the real world. They have made poker a fixture of the charity fundraising landscape.

Skill, Luck, Superstition and Rules

Even US presidents have used poker to raise money, albeit with different aims and objectives. Bill Clinton's charitable organization the Clinton Foundation runs twice-yearly tournaments in New York and Los Angeles with buy-ins of $20,000 per player.

It is a well documented fact that Richard Nixon bankrolled his first political run for office, that of a congressional California seat in 1946, from poker winnings. Nixon was an excellent poker player and won this money whilst in the Navy during the war.

FEDX is one of the biggest corporations in the world founded by Frederick Smith in 1971 with $4 million from an inheritance and $80 million in loans.

Unfortunately in the first two years the company was millions of dollars in debt and on the verge of bankruptcy and the funds dwindled to just $5,000.

On an impulse Smith took the $5,000 went to Las Vegas and gambled it all on the blackjack tables. He came home with $27,000 which allowed the company to stay in operation for another week. He also used the money to raise another $27 million and by 1976 FEDX issued its first profit of $3.6 million and a few years later went public and has been thriving ever since. A gambling success story!

The biggest poker game I ever witnessed was the Big One for One Drop, which takes place every two years at the WSOP in July. The entry fee is $1 million and with the winner taking $15million, it is the biggest pay out in poker history. The total entries the year I was a spell bound spectator was 42 players, and I still remember with awe, the $42 million piled up in $10,000 bundles at the side of the final table. The Rio's armed security team were not far away! All the players at the final table were 'in the money', the player knocked out in ninth place receiving just over $1 million. It was mesmerizing sitting watching these players, knowing that a turn of a card, one second of lost concentration, or one bad call could cost them $14 million.

Skill, Luck, Superstition and Rules

The final winner that year was Daniel Coleman a 24 year old American from Massachusetts, and the runner up was Daniel Negreanu, a high profile professional poker player from Canada who took the second place prize of $8 million.

The event is the brain child of Guy Laliberte, the owner of Cirque du Soleil, who himself is a very good poker player, and created the One Drop Foundation charity. $5 million of the entry fees were donated to this charity which provides fresh water for villages and townships in Africa. Whether it is $5 million by the professionals of Las Vegas, or £35,000 from semi professionals of Wolverhampton, or £5,000 from the amateurs of Blackpool, these events show the true nature of poker players. These events are not unique, Jerry Yang the 2007 Main Event winner at the WSOP donated 10% of his $8.5 million to three separate charities, and there are many instances other than those noted above; it is in contradiction of perhaps the general public's perception of ner' do well gamblers sitting around in secret smoke filled back rooms, cheating and swindling each other whilst playing poker.

Chapter 4

 Professionals, Semi Professionals and

Amateurs:

What constitutes a 'professional' poker player?

There are hundreds of poker players who play every day in Vegas casinos, some for high stakes, some for medium stakes and some like myself for small stakes. They vary greatly in their reasons for playing poker, and apart from the high stakes players I have played them all. Players who regularly frequent the Mirage and the Excalibur who I have become to know over the years; players who will recognise you and ask of your wellbeing whenever you walk into the card room. Small to Medium stake players like Kevin - Kevin was a truck driver for 20 years in New York and decided to retire to better climes in Las Vegas on his retirement. Kevin usually makes his appearance in the Mirage card room at around 11.30am each day including Saturday and Sunday. One of the reasons for this relatively early start is that the Mirage card room runs a bonus of £100 from the start of play until 1.00pm if a player has Aces 'cracked'. For the poker disadvantaged this means that if you have AA which is the best starting hand in poker, but get beat by a lesser ranked hand.

Kevin usually leaves the Mirage $3 - $6 game around 1.30pm each day. So, can he be termed a 'professional poker player'; or even a 'semi-professional' poker player? After all he only has his pension and no other occupational way of earning money. Would he would be classed in

Professionals, Semi Professionals and Amateurs

people's perception just the same as perhaps the bygone days when soccer and rugby players usually had a 'proper' job, and were just paid for the Saturday when they played the game.

Kevin did not play his poker like many of the young professional high stakes poker players I have watched in the Bellegio, Aria and other high end poker rooms.

These players sit quietly mostly listening to music on the smart phones speaking to each or the dealer rarely, grinding out the game. Kevin was a typical New Yorker, full of verbal communication which is delivered in that typical tough guy clipped style and tongue. I enjoyed his company and spent many pleasurable hours with him in the Mirage card room.

There are numerous examples of players like Kevin with whom I have played over the years, and without question all of them took their play seriously just like Maurice from my early Blackpool days.

These players may not be true professional players, but they approach the game in the same theoretical manner in that they try to remember the other players and the way they play. One year whilst playing in the Mirage I got into conversation with Tony a young Las Vegas resident, and talked of many things England and USA comparison wise. I think I played with him perhaps three or four times over the week. I cannot remember his second name, but did not see him on subsequent visits for around 3 years. I then met him at the $2 - $6 spread game in the Excalibur some 3 years later. Like me, he did not remember names, but remembered everything about me that I had discussed with him three years ago in the Mirage; both poker wise and personal life wise.

One very disconcerting (to me) incident happened in one of the hands in one of these later meetings in the Excalibur. Tony was not in the hand, but I held a pair of Aces (termed American Airlines in poker jargon), which is a very good starting hand and having got a couple of callers from my initial raise. I was confident of winning a fair size pot and was mentally rubbing my hands together. As the hand was played through, I tried to disguise my strong hand as well as possible, and the hand was eventually played out to the river (final card). By the end of the hand there were just three of us left in the pot and the dealer told us to turn over our cards.

Before I could do this, Tony from a seat opposite me said:

"I know what you are holding - American Airlines"

I was astounded and looked at him in disbelief, just by simply looking at my betting pattern during the hand he had read me like a book - and as I raked in the large pot, I was just pleased he had not been in the hand, and I realised how far behind these regular Vegas players I was. Tony was a typical low stakes Vegas professional, i.e., that he had no other regular means of income other than from poker. But the above incident illustrates exactly how good some of these small stakes grinders are in Vegas.

Over the course of that 2 week trip I had long conversations with Tony, mainly about playing as a part time professional small stakes player in Vegas. That is how he saw himself; a part time professional. His wife was a nurse at the Sunrise Hospital and Medical Centre, so with a good wage coming into the house this allowed him to play on a semi professional basis.

Like Dunn the other small stakes professional mentioned below in this chapter, Tony preferred to move around the different casinos in Vegas looking for the 'tourist's games', so therefore he mainly confined himself to the popular casinos on the strip. He explained it was a grind and that sometimes he had to take breaks from the humdrum rounds of the card rooms. But Tony was obviously a communicator, a talker and as he mentioned conversing with people; finding out all about them (including the way they play!) makes it more enjoyable and detracts from what otherwise would be a monotonous

Professionals, Semi Professionals and Amateurs

and tiring way of life. I had no reason to disbelieve him, and when I inquired of him amongst the other local poker players I knew - they all confirmed what he had told me, and he was well liked and respected by these locals in the poker rooms on the strip.

He was a proud young man, and made it plain to me, although he did not have to, that he did not receive any benefits (or welfare as the Americans call it) from the government. Of course he did not mention, and I did not ask, if he paid taxes on his winnings - I suspect not.

Another example of this dilemma of defining a professional poker player can be seen in many of the regular players who do have other employment and other incomes.

An example of another player I got acquainted with over the years is Eddie, a middle aged Mexican who worked as a chef at the Excalibur. Every night after his shift he would shower, change and sally forth to the Excalibur card room, set up his tablet to watch a film or video and play poker until around 10.00 pm. Eddie played his poker every night except Saturday and Sunday without fail.

The third of my examples of amateur poker players who could or could not be termed semi-professional is someone who has two other jobs/careers other than poker, Carl.

Carl is a very good poker player who plays low to medium stake games around Vegas, usually in the Excalibur. Carl deals poker every day at Bally's and then plays at the Excalibur in the evenings. Carl not only makes his money as a dealer, but also by playing the stock market, and can be seen going through his spread sheets most nights at the poker table. He is always willing to offer advice and tips re stocks and currency fluctuations, markets, investments etc to the regular players at the table. He would however, never dream of giving information on how to play a particular hand or poker strategy in general.

Professionals, Semi Professionals and Amateurs

Carl hails from New York and was a neighbour of Hilary and Bill Clinton, and often regales the table of his stories about the Clintons and their 'criminal activity' (his words - not mine). Carl, is a good player and undoubtedly makes money, albeit low, on his poker playing.

In my earlier playing days in Vegas I played a lot of poker at the Sahara. It was a well run card room with a variety of small stakes cash games and tournaments. They ran a great Sunday night tournament which regularly had nine or ten tables, and the biggest sandwiches I have ever seen free on the mid tournament break. I would often play in the afternoon $3 - $6 cash game and I remember vividly one player in particular. This gentleman would come into the game - never speak to anyone, but play in the most aggressive manner I have ever witnessed at a poker table. He very rarely called a hand, but would invariably raise or re-raise in every situation, or on sporadic occasions he would simply fold his cards - he never flat called.

Now, to the poker disadvantaged a $3 - $6 game may not appear to yield much of a profit, or in fact could be seen as easy to call these limited raises. But anyone who has played this limit game knows, that pots can easily and frequently do reach $100 + with raises and re-raises on the betting rounds. This gentleman would just play for around an hour, betting as per mentioned above. During my visits to the Sahara card room I never saw this player walk away without being $300 odd to the better. By any standards $300 for little over an hour's work is not bad!

I do not know if he was a professional in the true sense of the word, but he was known to some of the regular players, who would raise their eyebrows and sometimes mutter: *"Here he comes"* to no one in particular. None of the regulars knew much about him, because he never spoke to anyone, so did he have a 'proper job', or did he play in the Sahara and perhaps other card rooms in Vegas, to make his living?

Professionals, Semi Professionals and Amateurs

If we look at the other end of the scale we can add one more name to the other celebrities noted above who play poker, Jennifer Tilley (born: Jennifer Ellen Chan) who can perhaps be mentioned as a separate entity to the others above. Jennifer Tilley is a much better player than any of the other celebrities noted above, with perhaps the possible exception of Don Cheadle. Not only is she a good and ever present poker player but also a successful actress with a string of films behind her and appearances in *'Hill Street Blues'* and *'Cheers'*. She was also nominated for an Academy Award for Best Supporting Actress in Woody Allen's *'Bullets over Broadway'*.

I have seen her play poker and she is good, and I would suspect could make a very good living just playing poker. She is a World Series of Poker Ladies' Event bracelet winner, the first celebrity to win a World Series tournament and has subsequently won a long list of poker titles. Jennifer Tilly, like Maria Ho, another top class female poker player often wears low-cut tops when playing poker and one of her famous quotes when asked the reason for this was:

'To look cute; if people are really playing poker they don't care - nothing looks better than a pair of aces. They are not looking at your pair - they are looking at their pair'.

In 2005 Tilly stated that she was more interested in playing poker than acting, but by 2008 announced her retirement from poker as a career saying:

'I love poker but greatness in poker is an elusive dream. There are too many variants. Trying to find validation in poker is like trying to find a virgin in a whorehouse. I'm not giving up poker entirely – gambling is an addiction after all. I'm just going to treat it more like a hobby and less like a career'.

However, in 2010 she resumed her poker career and as at 2017 her live tournament winnings exceeded $992,000.

Professionals, Semi Professionals and Amateurs

If you were to ask Jennifer Tilley if she would call herself a professional or an amateur poker player, I am sure she would be insulted. She would without doubt consider herself as a professional poker player - but like Carl and the others above she does not make her living solely by playing poker. Although she maintains that it is a 'hobby' it can be seen from her tournament winnings that it must be something more than this. It is also interesting to note that she calls it gambling and notes it as an addiction.

The definition of a true professional then must be someone who makes his or her living solely by playing poker and nothing else. But would Jennifer Tilley and Bill Klien be offended if you called them amateurs? I suspect they would.

There are well documented 'assets' that are touted by all and sundry as to what a professional poker player needs to survive in the cut throat world of the professional game. These assets appear to be the same whether the player is a tournament player or a cash game player despite the fact that the differing game structure requires a different method of execution.

One of the major differences between the professional and the amateur is the amount of time and effort they are prepared to put into improving their game. Some of these are noted below by professional poker players, but an example of the effort needed can be exemplified by Isaac Haxton in *'The Pursuit of Poker Success'*, Haxton is one of the up and coming generation of professional poker players and he notes in his early learning process of the game. He was at University studying Computer Science and his University offered a class in Game Theory in Poker - which he took. This led him into discussions on such subjects as: constructing ranges, minimum defence frequencies and optimizing betting frequencies across multiple streaks, and other such concepts - *"ugghh"* - I struggle with calculating my chances of making my flush, i.e., 52 divided by 8! - that is why I am still playing small stakes poker then!

As an amateur player in Vegas it is important to know the level of the game you get involved in, and who the other players are. It is relatively easy to recognise if you are playing in a tournament that is too big for you. If you know that you have the best hand and you think it is a sure fire winner but are not willing to put all the money in front of you into the pot backing up the hand you have - you are in the wrong game. In general the skill level in tournaments in any casino can be judged by the cost of the entry fee, i.e, the higher the fee, the better class of players will be involved. So it is relatively easy to find your own level. In no limit cash games if I have the time and the chance I will usually walk around the card room first and look at the games and the players. If I see a table where most of the players have enormouse chips stacks in front of them - then I know it is not for me. It is not that I think they are better players, but just that I am not willing to risk that amount of money - it is much too high for my Vegas bankroll.

I remember one day at Caesars palace in the old poker room when I got involved in a game that I should not have been in. It was my fault, I did not read the screen advertising the games properly and when a seat came available at a certain table I took it. Obviously I realised my mistake as soon as I sat down, but not wishing to look foolish by getting up immedieately and leaving, I decided to play a few hands, play tight and leave as soon as my pride would let me.

In the course of time I got into conversation with a young Las Vegas resident called Dan who was sitting next to me. He heard the accent as I spoke to the dealer and we subsequently talked about the game in UK and in the USA and poker talk in general. He quickly realised that I was not there to make any serious money, but only a social player there to enjoy myself, and not a very good one at that.

"Look Mike", he said *"Let me give you some friendly advice - see those players -* he pointed around the room to about half a dozen other players in the room - *"Professionals - all of them - you won't see them in the magazines, or on the TV, but they make their living by poker - fleecing the tourists, be careful"*

I thanked him, and after another hour of tight playing I said my goodbyes and left with my wallet intack. There are of course many professional poker players who grind it out in the small stakes games in Las Vegas. As Dan pointed out - you don't see them in the poker magazines, you don't see them on TV, but as he pointed out they are there. Carl Dunn is one such player similar to Tony mentioned above and is outlined below and it comes with the blessing of Johnny Kampis from his excellent book *'Vegas or Bust'*.

Kampis describes Dunn as a 'charitable Vegas grinder'; charitable because twice a month he makes sandwiches and takes them along with cases of bottled water around Vegas distributing them to the homeless people along the Strip. A grinder because he spends the rest of his time playing small stakes poker for a living. Dunn had been playing in Vegas for 5 years, and describes the life of a small stakes grinder in detail in the book.

He does not restrict himself to any particular poker room but plays in different casinos; he states his reasons for this as to releive the boredom and monotomy. So he is not always playing against other small stakes grinders he will try every now and then to move up a level.

'It is not straight up', he says *'and you will have peaks and troughs - you have to me mentally tough'*.

There are of course many major differences between an enthusiastic amateur small stakes player and a true professional, but there are many similiarites as well; some like the love of the game have already been mentioned.

Professionals, Semi Professionals and Amateurs

Another feature of playing poker that is the parallel influence of variance in their game; i.e., the upswings and downswings over a period of play. These variances will of course be more important to the professional as they affect the amount of money they expect to win on average over the long run and the results you are seeing in the short term.

Professional poker player Phil Galfond says of variance:

'I was told once that you will run worse than you ever thought possible. Variance is a beast. It is not to be underestimated, but it always is'.

One of the causes of variance is obviously the percentage of luck involved over which the player has not control, but this will only affect variance over the short term. Every player expects this to happen so we have to get used to it.

Another of the causes of this variance in the game is your playing style. If you play a very loose-aggressive style of play then you will be involved in a lot more pots and will be consequently risking more money than your average tight player. The looser you are and the more risks you take, the greater your variance will be.

The professional who relies on poker for his livelihood must allow and plan for these certain occurrences and have the discipline to ride them out. To the amateur, although annoying and disheartening at the time can just 'keep calm and carry on'. If this variance downswing goes on too long the professional will either: exam their style and method of play, remain positive, minimize their losses during this period and sometimes take a break from the game. In *"The Mammoth Book of Poker"* when discussing skill v luck Mendlson notes:

'....luck will always influence outcomes, sometimes for long periods, and you must become a master or your own temperament.......'

And, as Annie Duke, one of the greatest female poker players of all time is quoted as saying:

'When you're moaning, all you are doing is focusing on things that were not in your control, at least you are not exploring whether they were in your control, which is bad. You're just focusing on the one piece of bad variance that happened. There's nothing productive that comes from it'.

In an article for 888 poker in July 2018, professional poker player and tournament coach Alexander Fitzgerald noted that tournament play is likely to produce much larger variance than cash play. If you play poker tournaments your variance can be enormous as the blinds in tourneys, are not equal throughout the game, so your variance could be positive during the lesser blinds early on, but negative during the larger blinds later on. This is why no high earning professional poker player can rely solely on tournaments - they must also become proficient at cash play where the blinds structure is completely different.

The life of a professional poker player may be viewed by others outside the poker world as glamorous and exciting, a view perhaps tarnished by films and TV. The James Bond lifestyle in which the professional poker player is surrounded by beautiful women, drives a Porsche or an MG Sports and lives in a modern, spacious expensive apartment in a desirable part of the city. In fact it is just the opposite and as Holden notes in *'Big Deal:'*

'People think it is glamorous but it's a very tough life'.

Holden goes on to explain that there are travelling and hotel fees which have to be added to the entry fees, and all this along with the general cost of living that we all face can add up to a substantial yearly amount, possibly in six figures. When you consider that only approximately 10% make it into the money in a tournament, meaning 90% do not, you can see it is a very fine financial line. Mike Sexton quoted in the same book goes on to add:

Professionals, Semi Professionals and Amateurs

'It does not matter at what level you play; you still have to grind it out, to put in the hours..........it can be so frustrating, so draining. You play your heart out, you play perfect you get your money in with the best hand, and still get beat. You have no control over it'.

The professional poker player usually eats alone, travels alone and sleeps alone and mostly living on the edge of panic. Feared that it will all come crashing down upon you, and you will be forced to lower you sights to a 'proper mundane job' until your fortunes take an upturn again.

There is of course the other side in that you are your own boss, you determine your own working days and hours, but as mentioned elsewhere, there is a big difference between playing when you want to and playing because you have to make a living.

It is difficult to explain to the poker disadvantaged the difference between the style of play required for either tournament or cash games in poker. I remember well that in my early days in Vegas I was more successful in tournament games than in cash games. This was because most games in those days in the UK were tournament or comps (competition) and my style of play was geared for these games. However, as the years went on I realised that in Vegas I was becoming more successful in the cash games - I knew and excepted that for the first couple of days in Vegas I would be losing in the cash games until I 'switched on' to cash game strategy and the way the Americans play their game. Now in my visits to Vegas I only play maybe 4 or 5 tournaments over the whole of the 2 week period and am usually more financially successful in these cash games.

Variance that is sometimes caused by luck rather than bad play is therefore identical in its occurrence for both amateurs and professionals, the big difference between the two is how it is handled.

Professionals, Semi Professionals and Amateurs

I would like to note another similarity that both professionals and amateurs suffer that can perhaps be associated with both luck and variance, that of the 'bad beat' (see glossary). It is of course more devastating to the professional than the amateur when the poker gods wreak havoc on you through this bad stroke of luck, but I believe that the immediate shock, horror and anger is the same feeling. Every poker player in the world experiences this on many; hundreds; thousands? of occasions through their playing career, and I defy any poker player to maintain that he has not winged or moaned about a particular bad beat at sometime in their life. One of the most said comments in poker is:

'Don't complain to the table about your bad beat - because half of them aren't interested, and the other half are glad it happened to you!'.

These occasions are of course more serious in a tournament than in cash play as it usually results in a loss of a large amount of your stack, or elimination from the tournament. This can be compounded even more if you are short on chips and waiting, and waiting, and waiting for those pretty looking cards with pictures on them preferably both of the same value - or the paramount starting hand of 2 Aces. Then when it happens, and your heart flutters and you cannot wait to get all your chips into the middle - only to see the chip leader call you with a mediocre hand and hit the miracle card on the river.

For a small stakes player like myself who is only investing perhaps $150 or $200 dollars in the entry fee and the chance of winning perhaps $2,000 odd at the final table after the initial feelings of disbelief have subsided things are not too bad. But I cannot imagine the misery of someone who has invested thousands in the entry fee and lost the chance of winning millions through a stroke of luck.

There are of course many differences between the approach and execution of the game between the amateur

Professionals, Semi Professionals and Amateurs

and the professional player. Some of these differences are obvious, differences such as:

The amateur will only play when the mood strikes them and tend to play for only a few hours at a time. The professional plays whenever a profitable opportunity arises, whether they feel like playing or not, and if the game is profitable may play for anything up to twenty four hours at a time.

Money management is much more important for the professional players. An amateur player rarely has a set amount available just for poker, if they win after a session the money goes back into the wallet and is spent along with their other money. Professionals will have a set poker bankroll, and understand the management of this is vital, and fluctuations in this bankroll must be kept to a minimum.

Professional players are not usually interested in winning every hand, they concentrate on winning in profitable situations. Despite popular perceptions professional poker players do not try to steal the blinds, or bluff at every opportunity. When called to make a decision in a hand of poker the professional is only motivated by profit, to them it is a business decision.

As noted this is not a book designed to instruct the reader on strategy and how to play the game etc. However, I think it is important here to note some of the mistakes that I made (and sometimes still do), which is in common with a lot of beginners in the game. Some of these common mistakes not in any particular order are:

- ❖ Playing too many hands: as an inexperienced player doing this gets you into a lot of difficult situations during the hand, that experienced players will use to their advantage.

- ❖ Not understanding the importance of position: this is one of the most essential elements of Texas

Hold'em. The player in late position has much more information to base his actions on.

❖ Playing passively throughout the game: it is not the right play to be passive in all situations. The other players will note this and take advantage of it - at times in the game you need to be aggressive and take control of the pot and the hand.

❖ Bluffing: Bluffing is a skill that is learnt from years and years of playing poker. It cannot be done at random and a beginner should avoid it, until they fully understand the tactics and the psychology of the game.

There are course many other mistakes that I made in my early poker days, and still do, but to continue would turn the book into a poker manual, and as noted there are many of these on the market written by much better players than myself. Remember? Poker is an easy game to learn - but takes a lifetime to master.

The beginner must also be aware of the 'Peter Principle - which is applied to poker by Kampis in *'Vegas or Bust'*. The 'Peter Principle' is basically 'that people are promoted to their level of incompetence'. The principle being that an employee will be promoted through a company until he/she reaches a level in which they are not competent - and there they stay.

So in relation to poker, the beginner must understand that eventually they will reach a level of play where is not in their financial interest to proceed further. Of course, there are the few that continue to improve until they reach the dizzy heights of a Phil Helmouth or a Daniel Negreano, but for the lesser mortals it is important to recognise the level that they are comfortable with, both financially and skill wise. As Kampis notes:

'Don't let the poker ego take over.'

Professionals, Semi Professionals and Amateurs

It is not only amateurs and beginners that make crucial mistakes at the poker table, and this true story is perhaps a good example to beginners to be careful with the words and phrases they use during the action of the game. There is a well known phrase in poker: 'a chip and a chair'. This saying stems from the 1982 World Series of Poker won by Jack 'Treetops" Straus (Straus was 6'7" tall - hence Treetops). Straus had pushed all of his chips into the middle of the table on day one, and lost the hand. He had done this without announcing *'all in'* to the dealer. He lost the hand, but when he got up from the table to leave, a single $500 chip was observed under his table napkin. The floor manager was called, and because Straus had not verbally declared *'all in'* he was allowed to continue. By the end of the days play he held $90,000 in chips; by day three he had $341,000 and was chip leader in the tournament. He eventually went on to win the title of World Series Champion with the accompanying $520,000.

So, beginners beware of your utterances at the table, they may count for you or against you.

I am not a good enough poker player to advise beginners but would ask them to simply note that you should treat all games as practice to build up your knowledge of the game. You should also be aware that as a beginner you will lose, and only by playing careful will you keep these losses to a minimum and look upon them as the price you have to pay for this education. The objective is to make this education the cheapest possible.

In his book *'Mammoth Book of Poker'* Mendelson suggests that the beginner should only play with players of similar importance. I would not agree with this; firstly it would be impossible to find a game anywhere that just consists of beginners or new comers to the game and secondly the way to improve is to play better players than yourself and if possible learn from them and test yourself against them. As noted elsewhere in the book, I would not sit down in a game that I believed was under my expertise level.

Anyone wishing to take up the game could do worse than simply noting this quote from perhaps the earliest publications on the game of poker Yardley's *'Education of a Poker Player':*

Yardley's Law: *Assume the worst, believe no-one, and make your move only when you are certain that you are unbeatable or have, at worst, exceptionally good odds in your favour"*

Another difference is the delicate subject of drinking at the table. It is very unusual to see a professional or high stakes poker player drinking alcohol at the table. Perhaps, the occasional bottle of beer but nothing more intoxicating. Of course the amateur game is much more different as most of the players are there to enjoy themselves and along with this goes drinking at the table - after all the drinks are free anyway.

I have seen many poker players at the table who are worse the wear for drink, but surprisingly, it is very rare that this causes any problems other than holding up the game for a few seconds until they get their bearings or sort out their chips. I don't think I can remember one occasion in my 30 years playing poker in Vegas where a player has been removed from the table through drink.

For myself, I did all my serious drinking years ago whilst in the Navy, so drinking whilst playing poker has never been a must for me. I restrict myself to perhaps having one bottle of beer, or perhaps on a Saturday night having a brandy - but that is as far as it goes. I never drink alcohol at the table during a tournament, and the above occasions are usually in cash games only when I will be sitting down for at least 5 or 6 hours play.

So, the eternal question -what makes a good poker player?

Professionals, Semi Professionals and Amateurs

There is a plethora of books, articles, blogs etc on the attributes that make a good and therefore successful poker player.

Many of these well documented elements include (not in any particular order of importance): aggression, patience, and ability to 'read' other players, a good knowledge of odds and maths, and years of studying and playing the game.

It is also relevant that not all great poker players play the same - it is not mechanical, and there is a great deal of the human element involved making some players better or worse than others at any required attribute. In his book *'Power Hold'em Strategy'*, Daniel Negreanos says:

'Not all great players play alike, and will disagree on the best way to play a particular hand, and that this adaptability to change the way you play is important'.

Good poker players have the ability to change up their playing style to fit any given situation. Someone who plays the same way all the time is too predictable, and they end up losing big as soon as the better players at the table figure out their strategy. The pros who consistently win big tournaments take what they have learned from watching the other players and develop a strategy that best suits the current game being played, and they are unpredictable enough that their usual betting strategy can be used as a bluff once in a while. Many amateur and professional poker players will tell you that there are technically right and wrong ways to play the game, but they never use the same playing strategy every time they sit down at a table.

The following few paragraphs are by courtesy of Lance Bradley's excellent book *'The Pursuit of Poker Success'*. The comments and quotes are from some of the top professionals in the world of poker, and how they feel about their game in relation to some of the more acknowledged qualities they have.

Olivia (Liv) Boeree:

Boeree comes from Kent in England and is one of the top female players in the world with many prestige titles under her belt. She gained a first class honours degree in Physics with Astrophysics at Manchester University and if she had not concentrated on poker would possibly have gone to be a Astrophysicist. She currently sits at number 5 on the all time female winners list.

Boeree's introduction to poker was through an advert she answered in London asking for game show contestants - she applied with the intention of paying off her student debt - it was subsequently revealed that they were to be taught how to play poker. She did not win the game show, but she fell in love with the game - the rest is history.

She comments on the characteristics that have helped her in her poker career:

'.....another one is competiveness. You can't be a good poker player unless you do have this literally cutthroat competitiveness'. Boeree admits that she goes a lot on instinct learned over many years of playing in like situations:

'Instincts are ultimately an accumulation of pattern recognition. ....conditioned behaviour.....you will have a stronger instinct about something because you have been there so many times before'.

Boeree confesses that although 'number crunching' and analysing her game maths does play an important part in professional poker, and she does enjoy the mathematical side of poker. She also acknowledges that putting in hours of study away from the tables has contributed to her success: *'I've had some really good training, some of the best in the world'* (in relation to her boyfriend Igor Kurganov - another top professional poker player).

Fedor Holtz:

Holtz is a young German player who now resides in Vienna and follows the Mike Sexton philosophy on poker playing at any level, as he comments on his game: *'The way I see success for me as a poker player is mostly just enjoying, really enjoying what I do'*. Holtz goes on to mention that:

'I think that being really disciplined and being stable (emotionally) is probably the most important as a general skill'.

Holtz along with millions of other young kids got into the game after watching Chris Moneymaker notch that incredible win at the World Series (noted above). Holtz studied poker along with playing chess and computer game strategy in his early 20's and he notes:

'I did not study when I did not want to, because that's what poker was about for me, was to never feel forced to do it'.

In another quote from Strazynski's Cardplayer Blog, Holtz makes more mention of how his studious nature and personal improvement has helped him to success:

'This is how I approached getting better at poker - small, consistent improvements in different areas every single day'.

The element of fun and enjoyment has always been crucial for Holtz even in the studying and analysing the game. Holz is not so active in the game now but remains a positive example of how someone can achieve great thing in poker and not remain trapped by the game, but continue to enjoy it on a more reduced scale.

Phil Helmuth:

Helmouth is an American player from Wisconsin who has won 15 World Series bracelets and is known in the poker world as the 'poker brat' because of his sometimes brash and uncalled for explosions at the table. However, people who have met him away from the table describe him as an affable, generous man who is always willing to help and give advice. Although I have never spoken to him I have seen Helmuth on numerous occasions throughout my years in Vegas, and I suspect it is the second of these descriptions of his character that is nearer the truth.

Helmuth like many professional poker players started playing poker at University (USA > college), initially to pay off debts whilst studying. He ended his studies at Wisconson-Madison University to play professional poker.

Helmuth is a great student of the game both in theory and in the analysis of his own play:

'From the time I was 20 and because I was making a living doing it. I thought about this theory, that theory, changing this, changing that, how do I get better, how do I improve at this game, who is great at that game, what are they doing that I am not doing'.

Helmuth also believes it is important to be patient - especially in cash games, and through periods of variance:

'So, it is important to wait through bad times, it is important to have patience. When you are playing cash games patience is huge'.

When he was running bad Helmuth would write down every hand, how he played it and spend hours after the game analysing his play.

Jason Mercier:

Mercier is a young American professional from Fort Lauderdale in Florida with some $19 million to his career earnings. Mercier comes from a Christian background and in his early years this caused conflict with his parents and with his own faith. In an article by Samantha Rea for the Christian magazine *'Sorted'* Mercier comments:

'Initially, it was a major issue. When I first started playing, I knew they'd be against it, so I kept it a secret. I played poker with my friends and didn't tell them, When

I was 18, I started playing online. When my parents found out, it was a big problem and it became an ongoing struggle between us'..

Whilst watching him over the years he always appears quiet, friendly and respectful at the table. It was interesting to read of his comments on poker attributes of discipline and emotions:

'......I definitely struggled with my emotions throughout losing sessions. I would break things, throw things and it took a lot of discipline and a lot of hours at the table......and realize that I need to keep my emotions in check'.

Mercier also notes other qualities that he has that are important for top professional players:

'I think that I am naturally good at games and strategy, and also maths comes very easy to me. I am also able to put in long hours at the table'.

Like myself Mercier is a committed Christian, and like myself he does not feel this is a problem in his poker playing. As he notes in the above article religion is one of the subjects that is taboo at the poker table, so it very rarely raises its head whilst playing. For me, my Christianity helps when playing poker in that it helps to keep things in perspective to me, helps me to treat other players at the table with respect and helps towards my viewpoint that I am there to enjoy, have fun and not there solely for greed or the desire for money.

Erik Seidel:

Seidel is an American player from New York and is from an earlier generation than the other players mentioned above with a total winnings of some $38 million to his credit; he currently lives in Las Vegas. Before playing poker he was an accomplished backgammon player which was an additional source of income for him. He cut his teeth at poker in the well known Mayfair Club in New York City at the age of 17. On the professional backgammon circuit, Seidel met poker pros Chip Reese and Stu Ungar, who were also passionate backgammon players. Ungar and Seidel immediately liked each other and Ungar took the young Seidel under his wing and taught him the strategy behind poker. The first time Seidel was really exposed to poker was a night at the Stardust casino when he sat behind Ungar and watched him play, and he notes:

'He would show me what hands he would bluff and stuff like that. It was an exciting thing for me just to be around poker players as good as he was'.

At this time Seidel already had a family and increasing responsibilities. So, he became a trader on Wall Street, but the crash in 1987 sent him back to the Mayfair Club. He decided to turn his full attention to poker and to become the best player he could be.

Seidel readily admits that he is not a studious person, but comments that for him it is:

'More of a matter of how am I playing' or *'How did I do'*

and looking back at the end of a tournament and analysing the decisions he made during the game. Even if he only gets middle of the road results he needs to be happy with the way he played, and then he is ready for the next tournament.

He also states that he has:

'Always had the need to get better'

and that in terms of competitiveness this is an important attitude, and he states that he also tries to keep humble without having any level of delusion or having a large ego. In an interview for Poker News in 2015 when asked the question if he was going to write a book on poker strategy or perhaps a biography, Seidel replied:

'I don't think it'd be a very good read, I don't really have much to say. I think it'd be a terrible book. If I ever do write one, nobody should buy it'.

- this from a man who has won $38 million and 8 World Series bracelets!

And on the question of poker celebrities in modern day poker he replied:

'It's very lucky we have people like Phil (Hellmuth) and Daniel (Negreano), people that are out there. In terms of

drawing peoples' interest into the game they're worth a great deal more than I am'.

A truly humble man, and another excellent advertisement for the game of poker.

In regard to the bad runs in his poker career, he states that it is important to have a stable life away from the tables, and in the early years he notes the support from his parents, and in later years the support of his wife.

Daniel Negreanu:

Negreanu is a Canadian player who is on the top of the list in professional poker player's earnings with some $42 million to his credit. He is an accomplished player both in tournament and cash games, and has written many books on poker strategy etc.

As a 15-year-old learned how to play poker and at the age of 16 he was spending time in pool halls, hustling, sports betting, and playing cards. Like many other professionals Negreanu dropped out of high school and starting playing in both legal and illegal games in the locality. After building up his bankroll he left at the age of 22 for Las Vegas.

Negreanu, along with other top players notes the requirement for a professional player to be competitive:

'I always wanted to compete, and I have always been competitive'. He also comments that a mental state is important in tournaments, and says:

'That he plans, and my focus on my mental state is where it needs to be before I enter a tournament'.

He makes sure he does not turn up late, he is not overtired, knows the structure of the game, and makes sure he has got the food he requires.

One of the other things he notes, is what he terms 'the coaching triangle'. The first two parts are concerned with the game:

'What worked today; What did I do well; What am I proud of; How did I do in terms of the plan I set forth' and

then the second part of this analysis: *'What didn't work; What didn't I do right; Where was my focus lost; What do I need to work on'.*

Then the third part which naturally follows: *'What am I committed to doing tomorrow; What am I going to do differently tomorrow'.*

Negreanu has many other interests now in the poker world, but still plays regularly on the high roller circuit, and although a little vocal at times at the table (he would say this is how he gets information on the players), he is another good advert for the game.

I think it is important to separate some of these essential attributes mentioned by the players above into those that are advantageous at all levels of the game, and those that are essential to the professional.

One of the points mentioned in previous sections and again mentioned above is that of enjoyment, and I believe this is essential for all levels of player - for the amateur it is obvious, you would not be indulging your hobby (sometimes costly) if you did not enjoy it. It is also essential that the professional enjoys his chosen life style, that included many hours sat at the table and many hours travelling and away from home and family.

Humility and respect for the other players is another desired characteristic for all players. In the most part amateur or small stakes games are conducted in a pleasant and amiable atmosphere, and anyone behaving in an obnoxious manner can soon disrupt the game, and in fact turn the other players against him/her. This is the last thing a player of any level wants at the poker table. In the high stakes poker circuit most of the players know each other well, and away from the table many are good friends and confidents, so this respect for each other despite the large amounts of money being played for is important.

To highlight this respect required for other players, and to also indicate it is important in that you never know who you are sitting alongside at the poker table, I would like to

Professionals, Semi Professionals and Amateurs

move out of the poker arena. Kerry Packer was an Australian tycoon well known for his gambling and visits to Vegas where he would regularly spend millions of dollars on a weekend visit.

This recording of events comes by courtesy of Marvin Karlins' *'A Chip and a Prayer'*. On one such visit to Vegas, Packer was playing high stakes baccarat and was becoming incensed by a foul mouthed player at the table. Packer asked him politely to stop him behaving rudely, to which the other player replied:

'Listen buddy, you obviously don't know who you are talking to - I happen to be worth $40 million'.

To which Packer casually replied: *'OK - I'll flip you for it'.*

There are other well known stories of Kerry Packer in Vegas, many in regard to his generosity that I will note here although they may not belong in this discussion on poker professionals. I have no authority to quote here on the authenticity of these stories, but they are so well enshrined in Vegas folklore that there must be some modicum of truth in them. I mention them for reader interest.

Packer was so impressed by one cocktail waitress he asked her if she had a mortgage. She said she did, so he asked her to bring it in the next day, which she did. The mortgage was for $150,000 and Packer paid it off for her immediately. Another time Packer accidentally crashed into a cocktail waitress sending her tray of drinks flying left, right and centre. To apologize Packer paid off her mortgage of $130,000.

One dealer was offered an $80,000 tip by Packer but respectfully declined, informing him dealers are not allowed to accept gratuities. Packer apparently called over the Pit Boss immediately and demanded the dealer be sacked on the spot. The Pit Boss fired her. Packer then pushed forward the $80,000 worth of chips before demanding the Pit Boss re-hire her.

The above recognizes one of the downsides of poker and other table games in a casino in that you have no control over the people who sit at the side of, or across from you at the table. In the case of a poker tournament this maybe for two or three hours or even longer. It is worth remembering this if you intend to take up poker and are of a delicate nature.

To return to poker; I also think it is important to separate aggression from competitiveness, a player can be competitive without being aggressive, and vice versa. A player can be aggressive without being obnoxious or unpleasant at the table.

For myself, I believe I am competitive and it has been my experience that the vast majority of small stakes players are also competitive. This comes over at the table by my and others reactions to losing pots, especially pots where they (I) thought they were in a good position to win. No one at whatever level enters a tournament without the competitive nature to win.

Aggression is quite a different element of play. I believe it is accepted by most poker connoisseurs that aggression is perhaps the most important element of Hold'em play for the professional player.

In "Big Deal" Holden makes this comment on aggressive play:

'No Limit Hold'em is a game that sorts the sheep from the goats, men from boys and pros from amateurs, as the prime requisite of a good Hold'em player is aggressiveness'.

In his book: *'Lessons and Teaching in No Limit Hold'em (The Little Green Book)'* Phil Gordon also lists this need for aggression as his number one criteria in five of his requirements of the qualities required for a good poker player. Others include two of the criteria listed above; patience and working on their game. He suggests that these are not necessarily inherent natural characteristics, but are things that can be learnt and developed. He also goes on to make an unusual contention that may be hard for the beginner to understand which I tend to agree with. As a beginner learning the game you should **not** be concerned with:

'Winning money; reading tells or bluffing; not about winning the most pots - it is about making the correct decisions'.

One of my biggest faults as a poker player is that I am not aggressive enough in pots where I am either favourite, or have good odds to be the favourite. I think this is one of the most important of the elements of the game often quoted by professionals and much better players than myself. Whether this aggression is a matter of self confidence as noted above, I am not quite sure.

For the poker disadvantaged I will explain the need for aggression in a hand. If I check or just call a bet, then the only way I can win is if I have the best hand at the showdown. When I open with a raise, or raise during the hand I have two options to win. My opponents will fold, or I will win as above at the showdown. There are many other elements of play that fall under the umbrella of 'aggression' in the game of poker, but I do not intend to discuss the pros and cons of them here - they are much better explained in other poker theory books.

I will conclude this discussion on aggressive play with a quote from the book that has become known in the poker world as 'The Bible', by the legend of poker, Doyle Brunson:

'The very best players I know are extremely aggressive....and I firmly believe that's what accounts for the difference between a very good player and a truly top player. It's the dividing line. That's for sure'.

The strange thing is - I have met Doyle Brunson and spoke with him - well as noted above said *"Good morning"* to him whilst in Starbucks at the Rio WSOP - and have watched him play many times, and he does not strike me as an aggressive player or having an aggressive personality, so I believe aggression should be kept to defining a way of playing rather than a natural human characteristic.

Professionals, Semi Professionals and Amateurs

Poker Trivia and Quotes

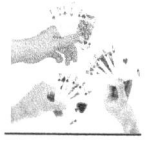

"Serious poker is no more about gambling than rock climbing is about taking risks." ~ Al Alvarez.

"Poker has the feeling of a sport, but you don't have to do push-ups." ~ Penn Gillette.

"They say poker is a zero-sum game. It must be, because every time I play my sum ends up zero." ~ Max Shapiro.

"Poker is a game that was invented by a Sadist and is played by Masochists." ~ Shane Smith.

"Poker is not simply a game of odds, moves and calculations. It is a game of controlled and exploited emotions including greed, fear, over-confidence and anger." ~ Steven Lubet.

When a player with money meets a man with experience, the player with experience leaves with money and the player with money leaves with experience." ~ Unknown.

"Poker is war, in disguise of a sport". ~ Charles Lamb.

"Poker is the new pornography. The Internet is awash with it ... it's banned in China and it's full of excitable Scandinavians." ~ Dave Lacey.

Chapter 5

Subterfuge, Collusion and Downright Cheating:

Another aspect of the game, and in particular when playing in Vegas, is that of cheating and collusion at the table. It is of paramount importance that the amateur or occasional poker playing visitor to Las Vegas is aware of how to recognise, and how to combat any form of cheating at the tables. I must be candid here, in the present popularity of the game and the experience of most of Vegas poker players these cases are very infrequent. The competition between the poker rooms in Vegas makes it essential that they are disciplined and professionally run. They need to do this to: make sure the players come back; the rooms are full, thereby increasing the rake; to protect their own jobs and for the reputation of the casino.

It is also of great importance that the amateur and small stakes poker player quickly learns the subtle tricks, deception and subterfuges that poker players will employ at the poker table. Again, I must impress it is not widespread and is very quickly closed down by the dealer or by experienced players at the table. However, the player who is new to the game should be aware of some these ploys that unscrupulous players will use.

'Splashing the pot' is a term used in poker when a player will just throw his chips into the pot without counting them out first, thus giving the dealer no chance to understand the amount of the raise or the call made. For example if the required amount was $50, the unscrupulous player would throw in just $30 or so - thereby saving

Subterfuge, Collusion and Downright Cheating

himself $20 - a good dealer would therefore have to count the whole pot to check the right amount had been donated.

'A string bet' is another poker term used when a player puts his chips into the pot, and then goes back to his stack and tries to put more in. For the poker disadvantaged - this is not allowed, the bet must be all in one motion. A player will do this for a couple of reasons. One to try and see other player's reactions to their bet, or to give the wrong impression on the strength of the hand they hold, i.e., try to give the impression they have a strong hand, when in fact they do not.

Some players will try this ploy in reverse, i.e., put a large denomination chip into the pot, and then try to take it back - saying to the dealer:

"Oh sorry I did not want to bet that much" or *"Sorry I did not realise the value of that chip"* or some such remark.

Of course, this is not allowed, but again it is done to give other players a false impression on the strength of their hand.

In the early days before the poker boom of the nineties when the knowledge of the game was less widespread, cheating and collusion was perhaps more common than it is now. In his book *'Geeking, Grifting and Gambling Through Las Vegas'*, David Sklansky notes teams of players mainly consisting of expert card sharks who, whilst not particularly good at poker, could manipulate cards, set up the decks and surreptitiously mark the cards. The honest professionals in Vegas obviously knew of these games and in which casinos allowed their operation, so they would avoid them; the targets of these scams were therefore clearly aimed at the home players and the tourists.

Also, in these earlier days corrupt dealers would have a knowledge of these games, and in places, be a part of the scam. Sklansky notes that most of these type of corrupt games were at the larger poker rooms, and he mentions the

Stardust and the Dunes. In my early days in Las Vegas I played poker in both of these casinos. I must admit that I did not notice anything untoward in any of the games I played in at these casinos, so either I was too naive to notice, the stakes I was playing for were too low, or simply they did not exist at the time.

I would like to make a point here about corrupt dealers. I have seen incompetent dealers that have influenced the game, but this was mainly due to chatting and not paying attention to the game, rather than any skulduggery. In fact I can give evidence of how the card rooms in this modern era expect a level of honesty and professionalism from their dealers. Just a couple of years ago a dealer who I was familiar with was dismissed by the casino for simply telling a poker player how to get around the casino rules regarding free comps (free rooms, free food and other compliments). There was no pecuniary advantage to this dealer, and he was a good friendly dealer in a well run card room that I have frequented over the years.

One time I did witness, and was involved in, collusion at the poker tables was in my early days when I would play regularly at Circus Circus. This was one of my favourite card rooms which I made my Saturday afternoon regular game. As noted before, in the early days the Circus Circus provided food throughout the day for poker players, and although it was not a particularly well run room, I enjoyed my poker there.

On this particular occasion I notice a particular pattern of play concerning players that were obviously locals. You can always identify the locals at the table as the dealers converse more with them, asking about families, vacations, local issues etc. The collusion involved these two players raising, re-raising and betting obvious non-locals out of the pot, and then checking the hand all the way through to the river (the end). It does not matter who won the pot, as these two locals were working together and would then divide the pots (after the game) between

Subterfuge, Collusion and Downright Cheating

themselves. This just did not happen once it was a pattern of play throughout the afternoon.

I did not say anything as it was difficult to prove - I just did not get involved in any large pots with these two 'gentlemen'. However, I mentioned this to the card room manager on cashing in my chips at the end of my play. The card room manager did not know me well, only by sight through my hours of play at Circus Circus, but I explained to him my suspicions on what was happening and added that if I had noticed it, then so should have the dealer. He gave me some 'scripted' reply about the Nevada Gaming Rules and that the card room must adhere to these, but gave no indication that he would look into the matter. I waited until he had given me my buffet comp ticket, thanked him, and told him that I would play my poker in future across the road at the Imperial which ran an honest card room, and left. It was the last time I played at the Circus Circus which closed down a few years later anyway.

Although it is not collusion in the true sense of the word, a bad or inexperienced dealer can influence, or treat as trivial, the breaking of etiquette or the rules at the table. An example of this was one evening while playing at the Golden Nugget downtown a young and obviously inexperienced woman turned to her husband, showed him her cards and asked him what should she do. Now to the poker disadvantaged this may seem acceptable, but it is strictly against the rules in poker. The husband was not in the hand, but I was and was astounded when the dealer who saw it all said nothing.   I said to the dealer:

"She can't do that, why are you allowing her to play the hand?".

"Well", he said "She is having fun and enjoying herself and it's only a 3 - 6 game".

The lady did bet with the hand; I did not have a playable hand anyway, so folded. But as pushed my cards towards the dealer, I said:

"It is irrelevant what the stakes are, it is the same rule for every game, and we are all having fun, but we are still playing for money - she is never going to learn the game if you allow her to do that at the table".

He was obviously not interested in his professionalism and just shrugged his shoulders. The couple were a nice couple and I had been in conversation with them throughout the evening, and yes they were just having fun and were not serious poker players, so not wanting to sour the good will at the table I let the matter drop. The dealer never did explain the rules to her.

I played a lot of poker during this time at the Golden Nugget and had witnessed this particular dealer before. This was not an isolated incident with him and it always appeared to me that he wanted to be perceived by the players as a 'nice friendly guy'. Unfortunately, he was abandoning his professionalism in the process and the good name of the Golden Nugget poker room. The consequences of this incident was that I very rarely played at the Nugget again. I don't suppose they missed me or my small stake game, but to me it was a matter of principle.

An example of a well run card room is the Excalibur; a card room that only offers small stake cash games and tournaments, but is always full with games going on until 6am in the morning, and sometimes through 24 hours nonstop.

This is a well run disciplined card room where I have witnessed on many occasions the card room manager remove a player's chips from the table and ask him to leave because he was annoying the other players to such an extent it was disrupting the game. On this one occasion a young American player at the table was disrupting the affable and friendly atmosphere of the game. He was talking incessantly and raising the maximum in every hand irrespective of the cards he was dealt, sometimes without even looking at them. Now, it may be thought that this is just the sort of player you want in a game - easy money.

Yes, in most circumstances this is true - but his continuous chatter and disregard for, and criticism of the other players was wearing everyone down. One by one the players requested a table change or cashed in their chips and left. When I did the same and cashed in my chips early, Eric the card room manager realised that something was amiss - he asked me why I was finishing early, so I explained the situation to him. Eric removed the player from the table, no arguments - you are disrupting the table (and in fact costing the casino money) - so please leave.

Alan the day time manager, and Eric the evening manager are both friendly, but at the same time professional with the commitment to run an honest and efficient card room with locals and visitors treated alike. For small stakes regular visitors such as myself this is a blessing and is all we ask for.

Whilst noting the roll that dealers have in the game, I would like to include some notations from Natalie Galustian's book *'He Played for His Wife and Other Stories',* which is a book of fictional stories with a poker theme. In one of the stories the narrative is in the third person from a female dealer. I would urge anyone - professional, amateur or anyone thinking of taking up the game to remember these words:

"She hated players who helped themselves to change from the pot".

"She hated bets not pushed forward, so she had to reach, putting more strain on her already aching lower back".

"She hated players who had keep being reminded to put in blinds".

"She hated players who leered at her and flirted".

"She hated players who blamed her for their losing hands".

"She hated disgruntled players complaining about their lives".

So, to all players, and wannabe poker players - don't do it!

Chapter 6

 Beginners at the Table:

One of the most difficult things for an experienced poker player to handle is beginners at the table. A regular and experienced player can spot a beginner within three minutes or so of them sitting down. There is a well known saying in poker:

'If you can't spot the sucker at the table within five minutes, it is you'.

It might be thought that these players are like manna from heaven to the regular player, but not so. One or two, yes but more than this number is a nightmare.

I was playing poker at Bally's in the old card room. Well, not really a card room, just a roped off area in the middle of the casino floor. The card room manager at that time, would 'ambush' just about anyone who walked past this area, and convince them that poker was a great game to play, and it was the only way to come out on top in Las Vegas. The result of this is that you had many novices sitting at the table, many who just seen it on TV and never actually played before. *"Great"* you might think - but no, for the experienced and skilled poker player this can be a disaster. One or two 'donkeys' (or bad players) at the table is ok - you can in the long run, eventually take all their money.

In this particular game there were about six or seven players who had been yanked into the card room by the exuberant manager to 'try their luck' A small timid Japanese lady sitting next to me was such a novice that she even had the hand rankings written on a piece of paper at her side. Another older well dressed American gentleman had to ask the dealer what to do whenever it was his turn to play.

The only other player at the table who was obviously an experienced player was a well dressed young American, perhaps in his early thirties. He looked over at me, I looked at him - our eyes met - and in that instant I knew exactly what he was thinking, - and he me. We were mentally rubbing our hands together ready to increase our bank roll and have a financially rewarding nights poker. I lost two racks of $100 each in the first 40 minutes of play!

These type of players would bet and put chips into the pot regardless of the cards they held, not knowing the odds and the general betting strategy of the game. If you are playing a good hand against such players, one or two in the pot is ok, you will eventually win. But, against five or six the odds are that one of them will beat your good and potentially winning hand - and this is what happened. After 40 minutes I got up and left, a lesson learned! I did return and play again in Bally's card room, but made sure they were experienced players at the table. It was a 'fun poker room' similar to the Flamingo were you could enjoy a good nights poker and conversation. That particular area has gone now, and is full of gaming machines - I often walk past those machines and think of the good times I had in that roped off area. They have a new purpose build poker room now in Bally's and I have played there a few times. It is more sedate and serious than the old area and most of the players are regulars grinding it out. One thing I do notice, is that it is never as busy as the old area on the gaming floor - again something has been lost and progress is not always for the better.

The above is one of the reasons that professional poker players do not like playing against amateurs. An amateur does not necessarily play 'by the book', and therefore lacks the understanding of expert moves that may be made to influence and deceive the other players. Neither do they play in a set way, thus not allowing the professional to get a read on their hands or other important aspects of play such as a players range of starting hands etc.

Another time I witnessed a similar situation with a beginner was in the Golden Nugget downtown on Fremont Street. I have played in the Golden Nugget on many occasions, but I have to admit it is not one of my favourite card rooms. On this evening, an Asian man of around fifty sat down at the table to play. It was obvious from the start he was a novice, but that was ok, the Golden Nugget card room catered for that rather than the more serious player, so it was not unusual. During the game I was engrossed talking to this young, very drunk, Texas cowboy - the real deal - someone who actually worked on a Texas cattle ranch, rounding up cows and things I had only seen on Western films.

After about 20 minutes or so I noticed the Asian man was on his third rack of $100 chips. Playing closer attention I noticed that he was asking the dealer a lot of questions on how to play. The dealer was very patient explaining everything to the Asian man, without giving him advice on what to do in any particular hand - something the dealers are not allowed to do.

After one rather strange question, the dealer looked at him and said:

"No sir, you are not playing against me, you are playing against these other gentlemen at the table - did you think you are playing against me".

"Oh, yes" said the player "I thought that when it was my turn to play, I was playing against you, and the cards in the middle were yours".

It was possibly the only time in that I have seen a Vegas poker dealer lost for words!

The other players at the table, except the cowboy who was so drunk he had no idea where he was, or what day it

Beginners at the Table

was, tried to encourage the Asian man to stay and learn the game. But after losing another $100 he thanked everyone got up and left, seemingly quite happy that he had lost some $400 in an hour and had absolutely no idea how it had happened.......... but had enjoyed it!.............**Welcome to La La Land!**

Final Thoughts

The journey from the small five tabled poker room in the Tiberius casino in Blackpool to the 40+ table poker room in Caesars Palace in Las Vegas has been a long and exhilarating one. One full of experiences, both happy and sad, of financial ups and downs but always taken on the chin and with a rugged determination to fight through the dark clouds and keep going in the hope that the crock of gold will be there at the end of the rainbow. I would not have missed it for the world; and would do it all again tomorrow. All sprung from a wrongly purchased book in the back streets of York.

I have enjoyed the poker immensely, but I think the characters I have met and the friends I have made over the 30 years has made the journey worthwhile. There are many other characters and people who have crossed my path in Vegas, too many to mention here. They all belong to that wonderful genus known as gamblers - risk takers - thrill seekers - whether it be for a few dollars at the slot machine, or millions of dollars at the poker table. I hope the reader has gained an insight into these gamblers and this wonderful game of poker and the wacky people from all walks and strata of life that play it. Perhaps it has changed some perceptions of the game and for the 'poker disadvantaged' to understand that it can be fun, friendly, exciting and entertaining - that is all I ask.

From the famous; the likes of Anthony Holden who has courted Royalty and Al Alveraz who mixed with Literary greats, to others on the lower scale of gambling life like the retiree Jake who sits on the pavement selling little drawings to help him with his poker finances. From the rich millionaires who play 25c slot machines, to the poorly paid waitresses and cocktail girls, and masseurs who live on tips. From the ones who are served with silver service

Final Thoughts

in top class casinos to the destitute and homeless living in drains under the city and beg on the streets for food.

All these people have made the journey with me, and I hope the reader has acquired a flavour of their being - that is all I ask.

'See you at the table' - Mike Connah

Tips: Visiting Vegas

So, you want to go to Vegas? - Just a few preliminaries:

Travelling to Vegas

Without doubt the easiest way is the direct flight from Manchester, Heathrow or Gatwick to McCarron International at Las Vegas. Yes it is a long and boring flight but with a book and a film to watch it goes remarkably quickly.

Over the years I have travelled both direct and indirect via Atlanta, Chicago and Los Angeles. Indirect may well be a couple of hundred pounds cheaper and be convenient for the last minute trip, but the hassle of running through the connecting airport; collecting and rechecking your baggage and worrying that you will make the connection is just not worth it. - Go direct, and don't go for less than a week - you will not touch the tip of the iceberg.

When exiting McCarran International you can either hop on a Bell's Transfer bus or taxi to the hotel. Both line ups are just outside the main exit of the airport. The taxi driver might ask you if you wish to take the freeway route to your hotel - this is the best way - it is longer, but because of the city traffic is usually quicker. The Bell's transfer is cheaper, but remember that it will stop at all the hotels of the passengers along the way.

Be aware that if you have travelled indirect you will arrive (and depart) from a different terminal than if you had flown direct.

Hotels

Of course the choice of hotel depends very much on one's budget. But, I have never understood many of my poker friends who go to Las Vegas and stay in hotels such as the Winn, the Venetian and other top ranked hotels. Why?, a room in Las Vegas is to sleep in and spend as little time as possible to occupy. The only little extras you get in these highly priced rooms are the fridge packed full of overpriced beer, spirits and snacks. Some of the hotels even charge you for putting your own stuff in the fridge - yes they have sensors in them to detect extras in the fridge.

My advice is to ask for a few things at reception. If you are staying for a couple of weeks, ask for an upgrade. Ask for a room on a higher floor - the outside hotel air conditioning units are situated lower down, and can be noisy. Ask for a room away from the lifts, to try and cut down on any late night noise of people returning to their room.

Over the years I have stayed in many, many different hotels both downtown, centre strip and bottom end strip. I have never had a bad room - all of them over the 30 years have been clean, all have had good beds and showers, all have good air conditioning, all have armchairs, desks and TVs, some have had fantastic views and all have good swimming pools.

You can easily pay up to $100 more a night for a room in a top of the range hotel as opposed to a middle range hotel - is it worth it?

Tips

When booking a trip to Las Vegas you must bear in mind that the hotel room rates will rocket when there is a big convention in town. Also, bear in mind the resort fee which will be added to your bill on top of the taxes and the room rate. As noted above the only way to avoid this fee is to gamble frequently either on the slots or the table games.

Eating and Drinking

Every casino has a wide range of eating and drinking opportunities to cater for all tastes and pockets. I find the buffets in the casinos the best option both for choice and value for money. However, most of the casinos also have food courts that comprise of many of the popular eating places for a lower priced meal, and all casinos have more than one coffee shop and cafe dotted around. A good place for a meal is in the American Diner type restaurant/cafe, most of the casinos have them; the American Deli is another favourite of mine, and again most casinos will have them.

The best place to drink is in the casino gaming floor bars which are lively and relatively priced. If you are gambling on the gaming floor, either at the tables or the slot machines, then the drinks are free - including spirit drinks; all you have to do is tip the cocktail waitress. This leads me on to a rather contentious subject in Las Vegas - and in the USA in general - tipping.

It is safe to say that the Americans view tipping in a slightly different way than we do in the UK. The Americans seem to tip everything that moves, and get annoyed if you don't. Personally I only tip as I would do in the UK, i.e, the taxi driver who has helped me with my bag; the waitress who has shown exceptional service or the poker dealer which is the convention when playing in Vegas. The people who work in the service industry in Las Vegas are very poorly paid - very. But, the casinos are making nearly a $600,000 per day on average - they should pay a decent wage, and whilst I keep supplementing the waiter's wages by tipping, they will not.

So, I warn the first time visitor people in the service industry in Las Vegas will expect a tip for everything - whether you do or not is your business. I think the visitor, especially if they are going for a considerable time, needs to make their mind up before they start - are they going to tip or not. On a two week visit tipping on every occasion can put quite a bit on top of your spends.

Getting Around

As the reader will have observed Las Vegas is a massive place and getting around, especially in the Summer heat can be a problem. Over the years I have told friends that the best free entertainment in Las Vegas is the strip bus (the double-decker Deuce) with people happy and enjoying their time in Vegas as the cast. There are ticket machines at most bus stops, or you can pay on entry but you must have the right money - no change given. I buy a daily return ticket that allows me to hop on and off

Tips

anywhere on the strip for 24 hours. These machines will take a UK bank or credit card.

There is a monorail that runs part way down one side of the strip, I have never used it so cannot comment. On the other side of the strip is the free monorail that runs from the Monte Carlo (now MGM properties) through to the Bellagio. There is also free trams from Mandalay Bay to Excalibur and Mirage to Treasure Island.

I would not have a car just to get around Vegas – it is too busy. Unless you know where you are going it is a waste of money and a recent innovation in Vegas is the casinos charging for parking even if you are a guest in the hotel.

However, if you want to get out of the noise and head for some of the spots noted in the book, then you can hire a car from most of the casino outlets - they will deliver and collect from the casino door.

Safety

Despite what you may see on TV or in films, if you keep to the main tourist areas you will be as safe in Las Vegas as your home town. The casino staff in Vegas are very helpful and I would urge any visitor that if you are not sure about anything - just ask, I have found that they will almost always go out of their way to help.

It is of course your choice which medium of money you choose to take - I only take cash (notes), but

Tips

whichever you choose it is essential that you keep in secured to your person, preferably by a chain or some such device. Most casino rooms have safes to keep passports etc in. I am not so sure that I would leave large amounts of cash in them whilst out of the room - I take mine with me with folded bills in a wallet secured by a chain to my belt. You can of course just take a Visa or Credit card and draw out money as you want - all casinos have ATM's - there is a small charge for withdrawals.

You need to remember that you are in the middle of a desert in Las Vegas, and if you are walking around for most of the day, then taking on board water is important. On most walking routes and bridges around Vegas there are street vendors selling water. I suspect it is only tap water, but it is only a dollar a bottle, and I have been drinking it for years with no problems.

Gambling and Shows

It would be inconceivable for anyone to go to Vegas and not gamble a little or see a show. Do both, but in moderation. If you are not a serious or knowledgeable gambler, as noted in the book - stick to the slot machines. There are many other gambling 'contraptions' and opportunities in the casinos for this - Keno; Wheel of Fortune; Automated Horse Racing, Bar integrated games etc - keep away from the table games unless you are

Tips

prepared to lose a certain amount of pre-determined money. Of course you may get lucky and win - just maybe.

Enjoy the shows - there is enough variety to suit all tastes - comedians, singers, musicals, circus etc. There is also enough variety to suit all pockets with gigantic theatres that seat thousands, down to the small lounges. The best way to buy a ticket for these shows is through the casino's own booking office not from the ticket touts, of which there are many, on the streets. Similarly with the trips to the Grand Canyon and Hoover Dam - book through the casino.

Appendix 1:

Ranking of the Hands in Texas Holdem.

Royal Flush   A-K-Q-J-T All of the same suit.

Straight Flush   Any 5 cards in sequence, all of the same suit. The Ace can be high or low.

Four of a Kind   Four cards of the same rank.

Full House (Boat) Three cards of one rank, two of another.

Flush   Any 5 cards of any rank; all the same suit

Straight (Wheel) Any 5 cards in sequence; any suit. The Ace can be high or low.

Three of a Kind (Set)
   Any three cards of one rank.

Appendix 1

Two of a Kind   Two cards of one rank, two of another.

One Pair   Two cards of the same rank.

If no player has any of the above, then the player with the highest card in his hand will win the pot.

Appendix 2

Glossary of Poker Terms

add-on   In a tournament, the opportunity to buy extra chips, usually at the end of a level, or when you have exhausted your buy in.

advertise   To make a loose play with the intent of looking like a loose player to your opponents.

all-in   To put all your remaining chips into the pot.

American Airlines
   A-A; also known as pocket rockets.

ante   Compulsory bet made by all players before the cards are dealt.

bad-beat   A hand you lose against all the expected odds.

big-blind   The larger of the two compulsory bets made to the dealers left.

big-slick   Slang term for A - K

bluff   A bet that conveys to the other players a bigger hand than you actually hold.

broadway   Cards on the board with all the suits being different.

board   All the face up cards that the dealer deals and can be used by all the players.

Appendix 2

boat — Slang term for a Full House

bubble — The position in a tournament that is the last one before the money is paid.

button — The dealer's button (disk) that denotes the position of the dealer.

buy-in — The amount paid to enter a tournament.

call — To match the other players bets - not to raise.

call station — A player who constantly calls, a loose player.

chasing — Continually trying to hit long shots.

chip and a chair
Phrase used when a player has only has one or a couple of chips left in the tournament.

check — To check, is to make no bet - when no one before you has bet.

community cards
The cards dealt in the middle of the table, for all players to use.

continuation bet
A bet made after the flop by the original raiser.

cowboys — A pair of Kings - K-K.

donkey — A poor player.

double up — To increase you chips by 100% in one hand.

Appendix 2

down cards   The player's two original cards dealt to them face down.

draw   Situation where a player needs just one card to complete their hand.

drawing dead
  Situation where a player cannot win the hand regardless of any remaining cards to be dealt.

ducks   A pair of deuces - 2 - 2

early position
  The two or three players to the left of the dealer.

fifth street   The fifth and final community card to be dealt.

fish   A player who stays in pots hoping to catch a good card against the odds.

flop   The first three community cards dealt.

flush   Five cards of the same suit.

fold   To discard your cards.

fourth street
  The fourth of the community cards dealt.

free card   A situation where no betting is made on that round (everyone checks) - so the next card to be dealt is free.

freeze out   A tournament game where no re-buys (below) are allowed.

Appendix 2

gut shot　　When you need one card to make a straight.

heads up　　When only two players are left to contest the pot.

hole cards　　The two original cards you are dealt face down.

kicker　　A small ranked card with a larger card you hold eg; A - 3.

ladies　　A pair of Queens - Q -Q.

late position
　　Players to the right of the dealer, ie; the last to act.

lay down　　To concede or cease betting when you think you are beaten.

limp in　　To make a small bet into the pot hoping no one will raise.

mid-position
　　In the middle of the table opposite the dealer.

muck　　The discarded cards, or the cards not in use.

multi-way pot
　　A hand that involves most of the players at the table.

no-limit　　A cash game where there is no limit to the amount you can bet.

nuts　　The best possible hand.

Appendix 2

off suit	Too describe cards of two different suits.
open ended	The situation when a player can make a straight.
outs	The number of cards/chances you have to make a hand.
over-card	A card you hold that is higher to any of the community cards.
paint	Any picture card.
pocket rockets	Slang term for A - A.
position	Refers to the seat (position) a player is in relation to the dealer.
pot	The total amount of winnable money in the middle of the table.
pot odds	Calculation of the amount of the pot in relation to the amount of money you have to bet.
quads	Four of a kind.
rags	Cards of no use to the player's hand - unplayable cards.
rainbow	Community cards all of different suits. Usually on the 'flop'.
rake	The amount of money the casino takes out of each pot.

Appendix 2

re-buy   A tournament game where you can buy more chips when you lose your entry chips.

river   The fifth and last of the community cards to be dealt.

rock   A player who only plays with premium cards in his hand.

satellite   A qualifying event for a larger tournament.

set   'Trips' - 3 cards of the same rank.

side pot   A secondary pot, usually because one of the players is all in.

sit & go   A type of tournament, usually played online.

shorthanded   Refers to a game with four or fewer players.

showdown   When all betting has finished, and the players show their hands.

slow rolling   Delaying in showing your hand when you know you have the winning hand - considered bad etiquette in poker.

small blind   The smaller of the two required blinds (antis) at the start of the hand.

splash the pot
    To throw chips indiscriminately into the pot to hide their value.

split pot   When two players have the same hand and the pot is divided between them.

Appendix 2

string bet To place chips into the pot - and then go back to your stack for more - not allowed.

suited connectors
 When a player holds two cards of the same suit that are in sequence, e.g., 6 & 7 of Hearts.

tell An unknown physical indication by a player that may give an insight into their play or hand.

tight player Someone who only plays premium hands.

tilt A player who plays illogically usually due to anger or frustration.

trips Term for three of any cards of the same rank - a set; e.g. K-K-K

turn The fourth community card dealt - '4th street'.

under the gun
 The first player to act - immediately to the left of the dealer.

value bet To bet large when you think you are winning to get maximum profit

wheel Term for the lowest possible straight; i.e., A-2-3-4-5.

Appendix 3

Texas Holdem

Below are the rules and conventions of playing a hand of Texas Holdem, which is the form of the game now most widely played around the world. There is no official governing body that decides the rules of the game, but most establishments now follow the policy laid down for the World Series of Poker.

1) Each player is dealt two cards which are face down, generally known as the player's 'hole cards'

   The cards are dealt clockwise around the table by the dealer, who will have a disk in front of him/her. This is known as the dealers 'button' and will be moved around the table clockwise to denote the dealers position.

   To the left of the dealer the first two players will have put in a compulsory 'anti' - a small amount for the first player, and double that amount for the second - these are known as the 'blinds'. The amount of these blinds depends on the level of the game.

2) There is then a round of betting starting with the first player after the blinds (ie. the third player to the left of the dealer). On all betting rounds the players can either: **'Check'** - do nothing; or **'Raise'** - increase the pot; or **'Fold'** - surrender his cards.

   If a player raises, then all the other players in the hand must match that raise.

Appendix 3

3) Three 'communal' cards are then dealt by the dealer, commonly known as the 'flop'. There is then a round of betting with the above choices for each player.

   These cards that are dealt by the dealer are known as the 'board' cards and can be used by all players in conjunction with their two 'hole' cards to make a hand.

4) A card is 'burnt' (discarded) then another communal card is dealt - 'fourth street' and a round of betting follows.

5) A further card is 'burnt' then the final communal card is dealt - the 'river' and a final round of betting follows.

6) The players who are then left in the hand show their cards in the 'showdown', and the player with the best hand wins the pot - the total amount of money bet.

   After each round the 'button' is moved clockwise round the table so as to allow all players a positional advantage in turn.

Bibliography

Alveraz, A, (1982)   *The Biggest Game in Town*
Bloomsbury, London, UK

Bradley, L, (2018)   *The Pursuit of Poker Success*
D&B Poker, USA

Cavanaugh, L *et al* (2009)
   *Ghosts, Gangsters, & Gamblers
   of Las Vegas,*
Schiffer Press, Atglen, USA

Coren, V, (2009)   *For Richer, For Poorer,*
Canon Gate Books, Edinburgh, UK

Dalla, N & Alson, P, (2005)
   One of a Kind
Atria Books, New York, USA

O'Brien, M, (2007)   *Beneath the Neon*
Huntington Press, Las Vegas, USA

Fischer, S, (2005)   *When the Mob Ran Vegas*
Berkline Press, Omaha, USA

Gordon, P, (2005)   *Little Green Book*   Simon & Schuster, New York, USA

Helmouth, P, (2003)   *Play Poker Like the Pros*
Harper Collins, New York, USA

Holden, A & Galustian, N (Editors) (2017)
   He Played for His Wife
Simon & Schuster, London, UK

Bibliography

Holden, A (1990)   *Big Deal*
Simon & Schuster, New York, USA

Kampis, J, (2018)   *Vegas or Bust*
ECW Press, Toronto, Canada

Karlins, M, (2018)   *A Chip and A Prayer*
Cardoza Publishing, Las Vegas, USA

Krieger, L & Bykofsky, S, (2006)
                         Secrets the Pros Won't Tell You
Kensington, New York, USA

Mendleson, P, (2008)   *The Mammoth Book of Poker*
Constable & Robinson, London, UK

Negreanu, D, (2016)   *Hold'em Wisdom for all Players*
Cardoza Publishing, Las Vegas, USA

Sklansky, D, (2020)   *Geeking, Grifting and Gambling*
                         Through Las Vegas
Not Known

Spanier, D, (1992)   *All Right OK You Win*
Mandarin Paperbacks, London, UK

Wilson, D, (2008)   *Ghosts at the Table*
Perseus Book Group, Philadelphia, USA

About the Author

Mike Connah was born and raised in a mining village in the North of England which he left at the age of 17 to join the Royal Navy. During the next 10 years he travelled to many different parts of the world and lived in Singapore for three years during his time in the Navy. On discharge from the Royal Navy he settled in Vancouver, BC, Canada.

On his return to the UK after some two years in Canada he served in the UK Prison Service for the next 27 years. During this time he worked with the whole range of inmates in HM Prisons both in the South and the North of England. After his time in the Prison Service he returned to the prisons as a counsellor where he worked solely with life sentence prisoners, many of them convicted murders.

After working in the prisons for a further four years he entered education and for a few years after his studies taught English to International Students at University. At present he works as an Academic Support Tutor with students who have Special Needs at the University of Central Lancashire in the North West of England. He has an BA(Hons) in English Language and a MA in Linguistics, four teaching qualifications and is a member both the Dyslexia Guild and the National Autistic Society.

Mike is divorced and has two children and three grandchildren.

Although in the past he has had short stories and poetry published, this is his first book.

Lightning Source UK Ltd.
Milton Keynes UK
UKHW010700200820
368545UK00003B/1047